# *Why Some* SEEDS *Don't Grow*

## 10 Principles for Parenting, Educating, and Mentoring Urban Youth

NEWTON H. MILLER II, PhD

ISBN 978-1-64300-736-6 (Paperback)
ISBN 978-1-64300-737-3 (Digital)

Covenant Books, Inc.
11661 Hwy 707
Murrells Inlet, SC 29576
www.covenantbooks.com

# CONTENTS

# ACKNOWLEDGMENTS

To my wife Kimberly who encouraged me to continue writing by convincing me that someone needed to hear what I had to say. I love you!

To my sister in the faith Karen who willingly gave her time and talents to help keep me focused and say what I meant to say. You are godsend.

To my children who motivate me by being so gifted and talented. Remember, you begin where I end. I intend to set the bar very high. I'm counting on you to raise it higher!

# PREFACE

As a parent of seven children, mentor of hundreds, and educator of thousands of youth, I have witnessed many atrocities in urban education that have led me to believe that in general, a great portion of our urban systems do not have the time to stop and truly analyze why some of their seeds are not growing. This book is a metaphor where the young people we are trying to raise and teach are called seeds and we—parents, mentor, and educators—are called the sowers. I do not claim that this book will be a cure-all that single-handedly turns around the blight that our urban education arena is experiencing. After failing over and over again in my own personal life as a result of some poor decision making, I have been blessed to master the principles that have repositioned my path back toward the glorious purpose and destiny that was originally intended for me. Although I'm not trying to sound mystical and mysterious, I submit to you that every person on the planet has a purpose and the gifts and abilities within themselves to accomplish that purpose. I believe that the fulfillment of one person's purpose is necessary for the next to begin the work that will catapult them into their inherent destiny, and this cycles continuously as long as we are on this planet.

Having said that, this book is not a compilation or analysis of best practices or techniques; it is a book of principles and belief systems that must serve as the foundation for any of the "what works" data that exist today. For many times, I have watched school districts spend hundreds of thousands of dollars on the latest technology or instructional intervention packages. These things always begin with great intentions and awesome expectations but somehow come to a screeching halt once they are introduced to the teaching ranks, and the professional development phase begins. Although there are many factors that may cause this phenomenon, the one consistency I have witnessed has been the foundational belief system of the staff as a whole. My check engine light came on in my car, so I went and spent two hundred dollars on a diagnostic tool that tells me the error code that the computer in the car displays, indicating what is wrong with the car. Awesome isn't it? I thought so, until the code displayed and I pressed the button to get the explanation, and I was clueless to what that machine was telling me to do. Immediately, it dawned on me—despite that fancy and advanced tool, beyond basic mechanics, I do not understand how my car works, and until that revelation occurs, I simply cannot repair it.

This book uses the metaphor of seeds and sowers; the law of the farm; the potential-kinetic-potential cycle; and rules the of expectations, cultivation, awareness, and crop rotation to stimulate the thinking of parents, mentors, and educators growing seeds to become respectable, productive, and contributing members of society. This book was written to remind us of the basic principles that exist as we grow our seeds to produce plenteous harvests. It will prove powerful to you if you open your mind to the symbolism and principles of preparation and work that we as sowers are required to exert in order to facilitate any kind of achievement in the seeds we grow. In essence, if you are looking for answers on how to better grow your seeds, they are probably already within you. You just need a paradigm shift in your thinking to seek to understand before being understood, thus enabling you to do the things your seeds truly need and not what your old thinking tells you will help them.

This refreshing and entertaining metaphor will help educators, mentors, and parents return to the principles and mind-set of the aha moment as readers ponder on the simple principles illuminated within its pages. The sturdy foundation one can develop by implementing these suggestions will only enhance any strategies or methodologies used to deliver content to any seeds being grown. In fact, unless we question our own thinking, change cannot take place. The state of urban education is dismal, and like the farmer, we are responsible for cultivating the ground we are given to make it conducive for growing and maximizing crops. Why is it that some seeds don't grow is a very valid question with a very simple answer that may not always be easy to activate. However, parents, mentors, and educators can operate in these principles and with a stubborn determination to do the work necessary to realize the expectation of a plenteous harvest. Submit and your seeds will grow. Enjoy!

# CHAPTER 1

## SEEDS AND SOWERS

## The Metaphor of Urban Youth as Seeds

I know this book is about mentoring, parenting, and educating urban youth, but I want to propose a different way of looking at those young people so we can help ensure they are positive contributors to our society. I am proposing that urban youth are seeds with the potential to grow something great, but for some reason, they are not growing and producing harvests as they should.

My premise for the seed metaphor is that we have great knowledge in the world of agriculture and have used it to produce greater quantities of crops, stronger plants, and even hybrid seedlings to suit-tailored needs we desire at any given time. Why can't we as parents, mentors, and educators apply the principles of growing seeds that we so effectively use in the world of agriculture to the young human seeds we are growing in our urban arenas? I know what you are saying—they are two different things; seeds produce plants and urban youth are human beings. I proclaim, you are both correct and incorrect. If you study the definition of a seed, you will find that it is an entity that contains the embryo or potential to produce a new entity. More importantly, producing that new thing is what the seed is designed to do and wants to do. Thus, our urban youth are human seeds with the inherent potential to produce something great, but we need to understand the principles that must be applied to help ensure the seeds accomplish their purpose.

In order to examine my philosophy of why some seeds don't grow, which again is a gigantic metaphor for the unnecessary stagnancy our urban youth seem to be experiencing in their lives, I have to take some time to explain to you some principles we have learned from our farmers about planting and caring for seeds so they can grow.

To set up the metaphor that serves as the basis of this book that states urban youth are seeds, I will use the parable of the sower and parable of the farm. Anyone who has ever planted a seed and watched it grow knows that they can't just put a seed in any kind of soil and expect it to flourish all on its own. In order for a seed to grow into a healthy plant, there are certain things that the planter must make sure are in place. Understanding this concept, I ask you to bear with me as I explain the parable of the farm and the parable of the seed so that I can lay a foundation for how and why I am comparing the younger generation that we parent, educate, and mentor to seeds that possess great potential and possibilities.

## My Dad and Mr. West

When I was a young boy, my neighbor Mr. West taught me to take a pack of seeds and pour them into a cup of water. He instructed me to let the seeds sit in the window sill for a least one week; the seeds that floated after one week were not good for planting. The seeds that dropped to the bottom of the cup were good for planting and needed to be kept in a cool damp place while the ground in which the seeds were going to be planted was prepared.

Mr. West and my dad were very good friends, but as men do, sometimes they rivaled each other. So as any young, smart, industrious young man would do, I asked both of them about the best way to prepare the ground for the seeds I wanted to plant. We didn't have a very large backyard and my father allowed me to make the garden only in a small six squared feet section, and this was the same spot that I was to use each year. That statement will make more sense after you read chapter 10.

One common piece of advice that never failed to come from both of them was, "You've got to get all the rocks out of the garden." I remember using garden tools like the shovel, the pickax, and the hoe to break up the ground and turn it over until it reached a fine consistency so I could dig my hands into the ground to a depth of about six to eight inches easily without pulling up any stones or rocks or other debris. I really hated that process because it was so much work. I couldn't understand why I had to do the same thing every year and why was it even necessary to remove the rocks in the first place. One thing I always recognized each year was no matter how well I prepared the ground the previous year, there seemed to be just as many rocks and debris as if it had never been cleared before. This baffled me, but because I really wanted a garden, I listened to those who I believed knew more about gardening than I did.

After preparing the ground, my dad and Mr. West showed me how to make rows so the seeds could be planted. My dad was careful to tell me to step back, survey the land, and to be observant of the way the water would run after the rain. He took that opportunity to teach me about erosion and emphasize how to make the water work for me and not against me. I remember this process required me to step back and actually account for the tilt and slant of the land. He showed me how to build rows that would resist erosion and ensure that the seedlings would not wash away.

Once the rows were built and designed properly, I was taught how to lay out the garden. This meant to decide what to a plant and where to plant it. As I said before that, I did not have much space in which to plant the garden, so I had to be very industrious in how I laid it out in order to maximize what was grown and eventually harvested. Once that was determined, I was allowed to get the seeds and any small plants that I had already started and transplant them in the ground that I had worked and prepared for them. One would think that the only thing left to do was to let everything grow, but at this point, the real work had only just begun.

## Parable of the Farm

Allow me for one minute to focus your attention on the work that has already been done just to get the garden ready for the seeds. This is important, so pay attention. If the proper preparation and focused attention to the steps of preparing the ground that builds the foundation of the garden are not properly and deliberately invested, then the seeds will not thrive and produce a fruit and possibly they will not survive.

You see, according to the parable of the farm, the preliminary things that are done are most important to the survival of the seed. My dad and Mr. West understood these principles. They knew I was not going to be a farmer. They knew I would probably grow up and lose my desire to even have a garden any longer. Nevertheless, more importantly, they understood that the principle of preparation was something I needed to master in order to make my life fruitful and accomplished. They knew I needed to learn what to do so I could spread the seeds of my purpose and destiny in a way to increase the probability of a good harvest.

## Parable of the Sower

Then there is the parable of the sower. This parable gives three different scenarios of seeds and sowing seeds. In the first scenario, this parable addresses a man who plants his seeds on unprepared ground, meaning no tools were used to break up the fallow ground. It was impenetrable, full of rocks, and covered with weeds. When this man spread his seeds on the unprepared ground without doing any planning and prefacing, he already sealed his destiny to be one of barrenness and no harvest. The seeds on the unprepared ground never got a chance to even take root. They were devoured and used for food by insects, birds, and other creatures. Thus, the fullness of their purpose was aborted and no harvest was produced. It has been said if you fail to plan, then you plan to fail.

A second scenario in the parable of the sower describes another planter who does a minimal amount of work and at least uses the proper tools to break up the fallow ground. This planter has taken the proper steps to envision what he wants his outcome to be and to plan on how to maximize his available space to make his garden look very presentable. However, this planter was unrealistic and chose to focus more on the outcome and what people thought of him and his garden. No doubt, he was preoccupied by how society classified him; he was more interested in the external or extrinsic and did not pay much attention to the internal or intrinsic. This superficial planter understands what it takes to be successful and reap a magnificent harvest. He has ample knowledge and exposure to many examples. He has probably witnessed and been a part of another planter's organization that is thriving and established. But this planter consciously fails to do the necessary work to prepare his ground properly. At first, there seems to be no consequence for his laziness and oversight because his ground looks fantastic. When he forms his rows and plants seeds, they spring up quickly and make everyone envy his accomplishment not knowing that it is going to be short-lived.

You see, this planter's ground is full of rocks and clay and toxic things so that the roots of the seedlings are hindered and choked and not allowed to draw proper nourishment to feed the plants. So the minimal amount of work this planter has done to prepare his ground was done in vain. His half-hearted energy and limited effort which he dedicated toward his preparation has only profited this man in the area of experience because nothing that he plants will mature and produce a measurable harvest. Thus, the only thing he has enhanced with his time, talent, and resources is his life experience. Sadly, that experience will never be activated as the planter suffers from a disconnected understanding, driven by the illusion he will most likely establish in his own mind that the plants failed for a reason other than his lack of responsibility to internally prepare the ground.

The compliments he receives about the surface of his garden and how good it looks at a glance help this planter live in denial about the inside job to which he continuously fails to invest his time and effort. Therefore, he who sows on stony ground is unrealistic and literally wastes his own time, talents, and potential. Although he gains stories, fables, and anecdotal experiences to share with all who choose to listen, and those who listen might very likely profit from the lesson of his half-hearted preparation, this man never positions himself to capitalize and profit from his own past experiences. This occurs because he simply refuses to dig deeper and remove more stones from the portion of soil he was given to cultivate.

The third sower plants his seeds on good ground. This man does all the things that the stony planter does: he counts his cost, he predicts his outcome, he maximizes his space, he gathers the proper tools, he sets out to do the work, he researches and gathers the required knowledge to accomplish this task, and finally, he attacks his objectives. The only difference in the sower of good ground and the other two types of sowers is determination. This sower begins his task with the end in mind; he literally picks a spot on wall and refuses to look to the left or the right until he reaches that spot. He is honest with what he has to work with and his character enables him to take the time and effort and resources to invest in any changes or modifications to the soil with which he began his journey. He is not afraid of hard work and sacrifice. His level of integrity motivates him to decide that whatever he does, big or small, he does it well or does not do it at all. This sower digs deeper and tries harder than any of his fellow planters. He pays attention to every grain of raw soil he has to work with and by any means necessary strives to cultivate it.

According to *Newberry House Dictionary* (2014), to cultivate means to influence change in an object from one state of being to a more refined state of being. The sower of the good ground has prefaced his task so that his soil is anxious to matter, and his soil receives seeds that it nurtures and allows roots to grow deeply and draw the nourishment needed for the whole plant to flourish. This planter has prepared and fortified this soil so that there is more than enough nitrogen, potassium, and phosphorus for anything that he decides to plant. Thus, his harvest yields a hundredfold and is very plenteous. This is all attributed to the simple fact that he has done the work to prepare the soil that nourishes the seeds. These two parables almost entirely encompass what is necessary to grow a seed—any seed. The principles of preparation and hard work are what carry any endeavor one sets out to accomplish a very long way.

The parable of the farm teaches us that planning and preparation in a consistent manner are basal ingredients when approaching, doing, and maintaining any task. Often, farmers awake early in the morning before the sun has even risen, and go to bed at sundown because there's nothing profitable for them during the night. The farmers' strategy is to maximize the time of day that best suits their needs and purposely replenish themselves during the night so they can have the strength to do the work that they know is required of them in order to reap a good harvest.

The parable of the sower simply focuses on the preparation, or more specifically, the differentiated preparation, needed for specific seeds on specific ground. Every case and every instance is different. It is foolish for us to assume that every plot of land and every seed will have the same conditions and requirements. Some soil are sandier, some soil have more clay, some soil are very rocky, and some soil simply lack nutrients. Given this, the parable of the sower teaches us to recognize the type of ground we have while we are working with it. It also encourages us to differentiate and specialize how we cultivate it so the needs of each seed is tended to according to the soil in which it is planted. Thus, if you are teacher, a parent, a pastor, an advocate, or a mentor of any young person in an urban arena, I implore you to study these two parables, learn from them and implement their hidden as well as their explicit messages in everything that you do while helping our young people (seeds) grow. I believe that if you intertwine your philosophies, beliefs, and experiences with the message these parables emit, you could broaden your insights and perfect your approach of influence on the young seeds we live to cultivate on a daily basis.

## Chapter Recap

Chapter 1    Seeds and Sowers
- Parable of the farm
  - My garden
  - Preparation
- Parable of the sower
  - Deeply prepared ground
  - Rocky, clay-filled, toxic ground
  - Unbroken ground

## Chapter Questions

1. What are the differences between the three types of sowers?
2. Which type are you? Why?
3. What can you do to become a more profitable sower?
4. Have you ever been a cultivator? How well did you do? Describe the scenario.
5. What components describe the parable of the farm?
6. Have you ever entered a task without applying the parable of the farmer? What was the outcome?

# CHAPTER 2

## POTENTIAL OF A SEED

## Potential has *Nothing* to do with Appearance

If you've ever taken physics class or studied physical science, you have been introduced to two types of energy: kinetic and potential. Kinetic energy is motion, action; it gets things done. When I speak to groups of students, I often explain the differences between potential and kinetic energy. I tell the students to imagine that over me is a two-thousand-pound weight that is being held in place by an invisible cord and at any time it can fall right on top of my head. I then ask the students, "What will happen to me if that weight falls on top of my head?"

Some students chuckle, some students cringe, but almost all the students immediately say, "It will crush you!" I promptly smile and say they're correct. Then I explain to them that the weight has the potential energy to crush me where I stand. That weight has the potential to abort my purpose, seize my destiny, and put a stop to my aspirations. I then ask those same students, "Do I look worried?" They usually say no and I tell them I'm not worried because potential cannot harm me. It's the kinetic energy that I'm worried about. If that two-thousand-pound weight begins to fall and I don't move out of the way, then I understand the devastation of the outcome. Therefore, I don't fear potential; I seek to understand and respect it so I can use it to my advantage.

An example of a group of people who understood that potential defines what can be are the slave owners of the Deep South. As a black man, I often ponder some of the reasons white slave owners did not allow the slaves to read and learn. One would think the smarter the slave, the more sophisticated things they could perform. The white slave owners understood the potential of those African slaves and that ignorance would support bondage that stifles potential. They knew that if those slaves began to read and write, they would expand their minds and begin to ponder different places and different things similar to those that they read about and develop a desire to see those places, do those things, and have those liberties. This would prove devastating to the slave-labored industry of our southern states.

So you see, those white slave owners understood the potential of the African slaves and thus feared what could happen if the slaves ever realized the possibilities of that potential for themselves. So they were diligently proactive in instituting strategies that blocked that self-actualization within the African slave, or at least they thought so. Once any living creature realizes what its true potential is, its inner man has no choice but to strive to fulfill the purpose that is defined by that source of potential. Of course, there has to be a conscious decision to walk in the direction which one's potential is dictating. Once that occurs, the pursuit for purpose is virtually unstoppable.

Potential cannot be defined by the size or appearance of a thing. Consider the mustard seed; it is one of the smallest and most fragile seeds that exists. Yet when it is planted and grown, it produces many branches and covers much ground, providing shade and nourishment for many creatures. A mustard seed has the dimensions of approximately two squared millimeters, yet the plants grow approximately six to twenty feet high and twenty-foot spread. Wow! If we look at things according to their size or beauty to predict their potential, we will always underestimate them and therefore never seek to understand their true value. Apple seeds grow apple trees that have the potential to produce thousands of pounds of fruit during its lifetime; acorns grow gigantic oak trees sixty to seventy feet tall that live for hundreds of years and serve as habitats for many living things. The point is, seeds have potential—great potential. This we must respect, regardless of their initial size or appearance.

This is a very interesting statement because it often drives the perceptions that educators, mentors, and parents have of the urban youth which they serve. We must keep in mind that urban youth are often exposed to daunting social economic stressors and as a result will not always speak with the most eloquent language or write with correct syntax or polished grammatical mechanics. They are often rough around the edges and engulfed in the culture of their neighborhoods because that is how they survive. That culture is easily identified in their clothing, hairstyles, body language, and overall appearance. However, they are still seeds! And none of us knows the potential of any seed at any time. Thus, it is our responsibility to ignore the appearance and to pay attention to the potential.

## Definitions of Potential

*Newbury House Dictionary* defines *potential* as "being potent; endowed with energy adequate to a result; efficacious; or influential." This aspect of the definition sums up how most people view potential. However, I believe this definition can be paralyzing or a hindrance to the average student simply because it's written in a positive note. Don't get me wrong, I believe potential is a positive word, but positive potential assumes a solid work ethic is in place in order to activate it.

*Newbury House Dictionary* also gives an alternate definition of *potential*—"existing in possibility, not in actuality." This portion of *Newbury's* definition addresses the attitude of many of the urban youth whom I encountered daily as an educator. A large percentage of these youth live in possibility. When you ask them what they want to be when they grow up, they tell you a pro basketball player, a pro football player, or a doctor, some say lawyer. All of these are great aspirations, but many of the youth who say they want to play a pro sport don't even play for the school team. Some who say they want to be doctors can be found in the cafeteria cutting biology class while many who want to be lawyers refuse to read the student handbook to understand those policies and procedures that affect them in their present school surroundings.

Thus, those same young people run the risk of being paralyzed or caught in a vicious cycle of marking time as implied in the second definition of *potential*. They actually live, exist, and act in possibility and not in actuality. Now hold on, before you close the book, there is nothing wrong with living in possibility if you're activating something to make that possibility an actuality. Hence, *Newbury House Dictionary's* third part of the definition of *potential*—"anything that may be possible."

Now I myself am partial to this portion of the definition since this part epitomizes strength, creativity, innovation, and just plain old likeness and image of the man upstairs. Now there is a fine line between the second part of *Webster*'s definition of *potential* and the third. The second part of that definition implies that potential is a reality, and the third part of the definition implies that potential is a reality *that can be*. I wish I had a dollar for every time someone said to me "whatever you want to be you can be," or "the sky is the limit," or "shoot for the stars." I would probably be a millionaire. In the same line of thought, almost every teacher and adult mentor whom I've come in contact with throughout my life has told me I have the potential to do wonderful things. Although I believe young people, especially those who dwell in urban centers, need to hear those statements on a consistent basis, they only speak to a reality that *can* be. What about preparing these youth for what *will* be?

Have you ever seen a child come to school with dirty clothes, crust in the corners of their eyes, hair uncombed, and teeth unbrushed? That same child is probably hungry, angry, depressed, neglected, and abused. Yet they come to school on a regular basis. I worked in a school district where there were no school buses. That meant that all children ages five to eighteen had to find a way to school. For many, that meant they had to walk to school in the rain, the snow, the cold wind, and scorching sun. The state requires a 90 percent attendance rate and a 95 percent participation rate at the end of year state exams. I believe this is a reasonable goal and one that is rooted and grounded in the best intentions for young people and society as a whole. However, I wonder how many people experienced living in an urban center or even considered the reality of the physical surrounding of our urban youth when establishing these requirements as state policy.

Let the record state that I wholeheartedly agree with the standards, but I believe we need to do a better job in putting resources and systems in place to get the students to the schools. I have witnessed the feeling of safety and comfort that many of our students feel once they enter our walls and walk the hallowed halls of our school buildings. I have witnessed—much to my distress—condescending attitudes, stereotypical statements, ill expectations, and hurtful comments by many of the educators who work in our urban schools, and those sentiments were often directed toward the students. Yet those students eagerly enter the building each morning, and for many of them, we have to tell them to leave the premises after school because they simply don't want to go home. The students' mere excitement and "want to" always made me wonder.

## One Seventh-Grade Girl

I once encountered a seventh-grade African American female student whom I had to discipline for cursing at a teacher, throwing her notebook, and literally ripping up some pages in her textbook. I was walking past her classroom when I heard the commotion. I opened the door and witnessed the tail end of the outburst. The teacher had her back turned and didn't know I had entered the room. I heard the teacher say to the student, "I knew you wouldn't last one week. No wonder you're always getting suspended!" I quickly walked over to the student, asked her to gather her things (I helped of course), and escorted her out of the classroom. As I did that, realizing the principal was in the room, the teacher changed her tone. She said with a very concerned voice, "I don't know what got into her. She's usually a wonderful student."

The students in the room began to laugh because they knew I heard her other more negative statement to the young lady. I quickly walked the student from the classroom as one of my objectives was to assist the teacher in restarting her instruction as quickly as possible. As I walked the young lady to my office, she cried, sobbed, and was rather expressive about her feelings toward that teacher. Needless to say, she didn't have anything positive to say. Once we reached the office, the young lady began to tell me how she felt that the teachers don't care about her and how they are always "getting smart." She elaborated on what amounted to be a lack of instruction during her classes. When I asked the young lady what she wanted to be when she grows up, she almost immediately replied, "A surgical nurse." I asked her if she thinks she will ever be a surgical nurse after being suspended from school as much as she does. She replied, "No! But I won't be a surgical nurse by doing worksheets and baby work either!"

I responded by saying, "You're right!"

As a parent of urban children and a product of an urban environment, I believe I have a responsibility to teach our students respect for themselves and others and how to stay humble and focused on their goals. Let me pause here to inform you that humility does not mean that one simply steps aside for other people because they think they are greater or more worthy than themselves. Humility means that one knows the power of their present position along with its strengths and weaknesses. Because of that knowledge, one is able to make a conscious decision to align their actions with the assignments necessary to pursue their preferred destiny. Humility does not imply that one thinks others are more than themselves; it entails thinking of others more often than one thinks of themselves.

Because of my responsibility and conviction, I suspended that young lady for three days for disrespect and intentional classroom disruption. However, from our short conversation, I had a visual of her potential, so I gave her an assignment in addition to the work her teachers were giving her to complete while she was on suspension. She had to write a three-page essay that informed me of the duties a surgical nurse performs and the steps necessary to become one, complete with a cover page, an outline, and five resources in APA style. Three days later, I was greeting the students as they entered the school, something I simply loved to do. This young lady entered the building with an upbeat giant smile on her face talking to two of her friends. I had already been to her house and spoken with her parent, who had to work and could not return her to school. She looked up and saw me standing there telling each of the children "good morning" and "have a great day." She asked friends to stop and wait while she dug in her book bag and pulled out her assignment. She proudly handed it to me, gave me a hug, and said, "Thanks Mr. Miller. Are we good?" Although I have seen that kind of turnaround hundreds of time before, I took notice this time because something was different.

Suddenly, it hit me like a ton of bricks—*each and every seed has in its purpose to become a plant that produces more seed and therefore fruit.* Because the planter understands the potential of the seed, a destiny is orchestrated specifically for that seed's potential to manifest into its purpose. That young lady doesn't show eagerness to come to school because of the state's requirements; she has already expressed concern over the lack of academic challenges and deficient sensitivity from teachers in some of her classes. Her eagerness to enter the building with an upbeat, giant smile on her face is driven by her potential and her ability to see the possibilities of that potential.

Every seed wants to manifest its potential. That is what makes it feel fulfilled, and for that reason and that reason alone, they will keep coming back. Thus, it is the job of educators, mentors, and parents to help the urban seed we are growing see those possibilities and keep them in plain sight to provide ample motivation to grow.

## Physics Weighs In

In physics, the definition of *potential* is the work done in bringing a unit of mass from a conceptual position to a certain physical point. The work done is the potential of that unit mass at that point. I wanted to include this definition based on physics simply because physics relies only on principles and laws.

I see a direct mapping between the potential of every child and every adult to the definitions of potential energy and Newtonian potential upon which physics is based. For instance, picture the space shuttle on a voyage in outer space. Suppose the National Aeronautics and Space Administration (NASA) wishes to bring the space shuttle to a point close to the moon so the astronauts can take some special readings on the moon's surface. In order for the space shuttle to get from that spot in far outer space to the point close to the moon, where NASA wants it to be, some work has to be done.

Now, everyone on the engineering team believes that the space shuttle can reach that point defined by NASA. So belief is not an issue. There is no doubt that the space shuttle can get there, and NASA has given the computers the specific coordinates and correct information to reach the pre-determined spot. However, the space shuttle must do the work to reach its intended destination. Therefore, when the space shuttle actually does the work to reach the point defined by NASA, its potential turns into active or kinetic energy until it reaches its goal where it then has demonstrated the potential to accomplish the mission set forth by NASA, its creator.

## Potential-Kinetic-Potential Cycle

If I haven't lost you yet, let me transform this analogy into goals and aspirations. Suppose a student wishes to be civil engineer and every teacher says that, without a shadow of a doubt, this student possesses the potential aptitude in math and science to accomplish this goal. Despite the fact that the certified professional opinions of all the educators and adult mentors in the life of that student have confirmed his or her aspiration is in fact attainable, that student (seed) has the responsibility to transform his or her potential into kinetic energy (do the work) to make their goal a reality.

This principle exists in every grade level: elementary, secondary, bachelor's level, graduate school, and on each project encountered in the work force. The important thing to teach our seeds who want to activate their potential is that for each goal they want to accomplish, it takes some work to get there. Knowing what that work entails will bring them to a crossroad where their perceived potential to accomplish their goals will motivate them to do something that transforms their potential into kinetic. Once this occurs, accomplishing their assignment is no longer conceptual; it becomes tangible and the seed we have been trying to grow begins to sprout roots and seek nourishment on its own.

This transformative follow-through allows them to engage what was once conceptual potential and turn it into something kinetic to accomplish the assignments that move them toward their preferred destiny on the level which they presently exist. Ultimately, this process just moves them up one rung on the ladder where they encounter their next challenge or task, and the potential-kinetic-potential cycle begins again.

As parents, mentors, and educators of urban youth, it is your responsibility to find ways to facilitate the stimulation of our seeds so they are motivated to transform their potential energy (dreams) into their kinetic energy (actuality). Thus, they can reach the next level of their journey where their next encounter with potential awaits them.

## Chapter Recap

Chapter 2    Potential of a Seed
- Potential vs. Kinetic
- Potential Defined
  - Possibilities not Actuality.
  - Anything that may be possible
  - Endowed with energy.
- Potential as a driving force to press toward the prize despite all hindrances
- The potential-kinetic-potential cycle
- With potential comes responsibility

## Chapter Questions

1. Describe a seed you are responsible for? What potential do you see in them?
2. What indicators suggest the seed you are growing possess a potential that they might not yet realize themselves?
3. Tell of experiences with the "potential – kinetic – potential cycles" that you have recognized in your own life, or in the lives of young seeds that you have mentors, educated, or parented.

# SPECIFIC SEEDS REQUIRE SPECIFIC NEEDS

## If Mother Nature Does It, Shouldn't We?

P lants are an important food source for animals. Like all other organisms, they have developed unique strategies for reproduction. Most plants produce seeds that are actually little plants waiting to grow but have the capacity to wait a long time before they begin their growth cycle.

When we deal with the students in our classes or our children in our homes, we should always keep in mind that they are little plants or seeds that are unique and have different requirements for their survival and progress. In order to further illustrate this point, I will utilize some of my science background to emphasize differences in the types of seeds and show parallels and comparisons in how nature cares for the seeds she has committed to growing. Hopefully, this will shed more light on the fact that we must differentiate our approaches when dealing with the seeds in our classrooms and homes. After all, if Mother Nature does it, shouldn't we?

In the biomes of this planet, seeds are scattered by wind, water, animals, or propulsion. Animals may spread seeds by a variety of ways such as by eating hard seeds, which pass through the animal's digestive system unharmed, or by picking up seeds on their coats and feathers and dropping them as they move from one area to another. As parents, educators, mentors, and community members, we are tasked with a very important job—to spread seeds. Every time a student sits in the classroom with me, I realize that I am about to do something for each human being in that room that cannot be undone. I'm about to plant, spread, germinate, or water a seed.

Now in the education realm, there are many methodologies and instructional techniques that are applicable in the classroom. This book is not about instructional techniques or methodologies; it is not about graphic organizers, classroom management, planning and accounting systems for gathering best practiced lessons, interventions, or cultures of assessment. This book is purposed to point out some of the principle-centered focuses that anyone faces when helping to grow productive human beings. It is simply about the mind-set parents, educators, mentors, and community members must have in order to help our young people grow.

But we must accept that just as seeds are scattered by several different methods, so is information, counsel, and instruction. Some of the seeds that are scattered by the wind are so light in weight that they get caught in the jet stream and travel for hundreds of miles before landing on good soil. Some of the students who have sat in desks in front of me have seemingly grasped the concepts of algebra or geometry or physics or general science that I have taught them, and on the contrary, many who sat in front of me seemingly did not grasp much those same concepts at all. However, as years have passed, I have seen some of those students that I thought would have tremendous difficulty successfully negotiating a four-year college program, thriving in their later years of college, and some experiencing awesome accolades within their career choices. Thus, I must conclude a delayed germination process took place in which the seeds of knowledge and of motivation took some time to take root in the lives of those students. Maybe they had to travel through the symbolic jet stream winds of their lives for some time before landing on good ground and beginning to grow.

## Types of Seeds

Nature's propulsion method of spreading seeds has always fascinated me. It occurs when a seed covering opens in such a way that the seed shoots out. Many of my friends and I have lived in urban areas where we have encountered some physical and social obstacles. Growing up in the ' 70s was somewhat frustrating; being considered a young adult in the '80s left us to really grow up in the '90s. The prejudices and battles that were prevalent in society during those decades communicated some specific messages to us little black kids with parents who sacrificed so we can have a better life. Our parents understood how we were viewed by some people in this country and were forced to prepare us for some disappointments, hurt, and pain that they knew was lying in wait for us as we matured and developed into adulthood.

My father was born in Durham, North Carolina, in 1926. The experience and wisdom he brought to the table of my life were so vast that now at fifty-one years old, I am just tapping into the true meaning of much of what he has taught me. One thing he used to say to me due to the climate of racial tension of his time was "If the white child gets a B on the test, you have to get an A just to be recognized. When the white child gets a pat on the back for his 90 percent effort, you have to give 110 percent effort just to be recognized."

Now, if you don't know my father and you judge him based on those statements, you may conclude that he was a racist man. He was not racist, but based upon the dispensational truth of his time, he was a realist. Because of his experiences, he felt obligated to teach me how to stay motivated from within. You see, his statements were not designed to make me dislike another ethnicity or race of people, nor were they to make me feel sorry for myself. Instead, they were designed to make me understand why some things in life happen the way they do and how I could overcome them to achieve fulfillment. When I ponder that one principle my father taught me, I realize that he was promoting the propulsion method. He was simply telling me that when I'm given the chance, aggressively open up and shoot out as many seeds as I can, as far as I can, to catapult my contribution to society through any and all barriers and hindrances.

In many cases, it is possible to look at a seed and figure out which method of spreading is used. For instance, if a seed has feathery extensions like dandelions, then it can sail through the wind, looking for a suitable place to germinate (grow). The protective seed coat, food storage area, and partially developed plant can all be seen reasonably well in a pea, bean, or peanut seed.

A corn seed is constructed differently and is a perfect illustration that not all seeds are the same. There are many theories about differences in education: Some believe there should be separate male and female classes. Some believe people of color learn differently than the white subgroup. Meanwhile, some believe the socioeconomically distressed student is not capable of attaining the understanding a well-to-do suburban student can. The plethora of existing literature in the forms of dissertations, theses, research projects, empirical studies, and meta-analyses create a tangled web of contradicting information about these theories. I do not disdain any of those statements; rather, I invite them. *The law of nature and law of the seed teach us that specific seeds require specific needs.* Some believe there is truth and falsehood in all of those statements, but the approach in addressing the statements far outweighs the importance of the comparisons presented. Thus, we must do as the planter does with a seed—look at it and examine it to better determine how it works so we can work with it and not against it.

Germination is the process that occurs when a seed actually begins to grow into a plant. The first step in seed germination is the absorption of water through a small opening called the micropyle. The introduction of water through the pore causes the seed to swell. Many seeds will swell dramatically as the water enters, and you will notice a sweet, almost fermenting odor in the water after seeds have been soaked overnight. This is from an enzyme reaction.

When do children actually begin to grow into productive adults? When do they actually begin to fulfill their purpose and realize their destiny? Is it in their primary years? Is it during their elementary education, or is it in high school? Does it happen when they are thirty years old and their frontal lobe is fully developed? That's just it; we don't know. So if we are in the position as a planter or seeder, we have to make our mind up to pour water into the micropyle of every seed within our reach, every chance we get. This is no easy task.

I worked in urban schools, and sometimes, hallway behavior can become quite festive. It becomes increasingly difficult to be nurturing and focusing on feeding and germinating seeds when there are three hundred children in one hallway slamming lockers, talking loudly, and grabbing each other as if they were out on the football field. But the very fact that educators in the schools I lead act as a planter and step into the middle of the hallway and redirect inappropriate behavior, address excessive noise, and insist upon young lady- and gentlemanlike behavior defines germination. There's nothing more satisfying than watching middle school students, eighth graders in particular, as they walk through the maturing process.

At one point in my career, I had the awesome opportunity to visit the high school in our school district periodically to serve as a substitute administrator. It is tremendously delightful to see the ninth-grade students at lunch walking in the hallways with such maturity and sense of focus when the year before in middle school, I had to speak to them over and over again concerning their conduct and character with seemingly no positive change. Lo and behold, months later, the students know how to sit in a cafeteria and have a civil conversation with each other using an indoor voice and showing responsibility and care for their building by cleaning up after themselves. Wow! If that's not growth, then I don't know what is.

From my vantage point, this is a great accomplishment, but the high school teacher has a different and more advanced set of competencies they are measuring the freshman against. To them, this is just the beginning of a journey toward young adulthood and nowhere near what a mature senior will look like three years later. This constant pressure on the student stimulates well-defined expectations and a positive trajectory of growth. However, for me, the opportunity to serve as a substitute administrator afforded me the opportunity to see the seeds swell from the watering of the many planters they have come in contact with up until this point in their lives. The experience was always quite motivating.

So far, we talked about two types of seed—bean seeds and corn seeds. Although both of those seeds are rather large and are made up of mostly reserved food for the initial growth of the plant, they are shaped differently and absorb water from different locations on their surface. There is another major type of seed that is found commonly on ferns. It goes without saying that we will encounter some people who do not fall within the majority. There will be some seeds that appear different and operate differently than the most commonly recognized types of seed.

Ferns reproduce through primitive "seeds" called spores which are produced by the small bumps on the back of older leaves. The tiny dark-brown spores are single cells that will develop into plants if they land on ground that has been prepared by Mother Nature for their growth. There are some students whom we serve who may require more accommodations and varied instruction, or maybe their surroundings have to include or exclude certain conditions in order for learning to take place. Those students are our ferns. Ferns are beautiful plants, but they are fragile plants.

There is a female seventh-grade special education teacher whose class I would walk through quite often. I believe her class has scored the lowest on the standardized batteries that rank them according to academic ability level in the state. Yet when I walk into this teacher's class, I am always amazed with the level of questioning and interaction between her and the students. Her class is a safe place, one that I believe she has been deliberately designing and creating for many years based on her observations of the needs of the seeds she is growing. She has done the work to make the soil in her classroom good ground so that even the most fragile spores that are assigned to her classroom land in the perfect environment. Seeds are more likely to produce plants in environments that are less than perfect. This particular school had a special education population of approximately 23 percent, and since federal law requires a least restrictive environment, a variety of special education services exist in the curriculum that the school offers.

Reproduction of the fragile ferns teaches us that these differentiated special education classrooms that are driven by individual accommodations to help each student be as successful as possible are necessary. The other 77 percent of students are seeds, not spores, and as a part of their inherited design, they have a bank of reserve food upon which they can survive and even thrive in conditions that are less than perfect. But this is not so for the spores. In nature, spore-producing plants produce tremendous numbers of spores in order to have only a few develop into thriving plants. Because we are human beings and have the ability to think on a higher level, we have created diverse environments that are more conducive for developing those students who are different types of seeds into productive and contributing plants.

Since we're dealing with human beings, this is a social science, and social sciences are not exact. Therefore, what happens when a child that we're dealing with is not one certain type of seed? Is it possible that a child has bean-like, corn-like, and fern-like qualities all at the same time? It most certainly is. In fact, it is very realistic that out of a class of twenty-five students, fifteen of them will not fall into any one classification of learners. Most of the students and children whom you mentor will call for differentiated approaches in your instructional technique and personality approach and even tiered-outcome expectations.

When we learn to notice seed types and the types of soil in which those seeds thrive, how they absorb the nourishment, and the conditions they require for maximum growth, then and only then can we prescribe and create comprehensive, nurturing environments that will help ensure maximized development for the seeds we are planting.

## The Seeds in Our House

My wife and I have a blended family with seven children ranging from ages of thirty-two to twenty-five. I have been blessed to be a partner in raising five of our children in the same household with my wife. I can tell you that each of them is very different. Although I believe that they are all talented and capable of accomplishing whatever they put their minds to, I still have found that the hardest part of my job is not guiding or motivating them but finding out *how* to individually guide and motivate each of them.

My oldest daughter is a very sensitive and emotionally in tuned young lady; she is quite in touch with her feelings and the feelings of others. Her emotional intelligence is off the charts! Because of her sensitivity, she is also a very caring person who is usually more concerned about others than herself. She was in Germany when she began starting a family of her own, and I imagine that was one of the most difficult things she has had to do in her life. I derive that conclusion because of her emotional intelligence; her comfort zone is close to her family. We understand that she is very discerning, and we compensate automatically.

As a father or planter, I needed to understand her qualities as a seed so I could help steer her in directions that match her inherent abilities, as well as provide scenarios and conditions to help her grow and stay strong when she leaves from our familiar surroundings. She is a very gifted singer, dancer, writer, actress; she creates soaps, lotions, fragrances; she sews; and she creates very tasty gourmet meals, to name a few of her talents. Knowing her qualities and gifts, we have tried to expose her to the performing arts and communications-driven activities. This was easy because her mother also shares some of the same gifts and abilities. However, because of her astute emotional awareness, we were careful to constantly pour into her and tell her how great she was. Not only that, but we were present at, supported and participated in as many of her activities as we could.

My oldest son is very athletic, musically inclined, awesome in the performing arts, and tremendously analytical. He is a very confident young man and tends to attack tasks from an intrinsic perspective. I remember one time when he was about fourteen years old, we were all in the living room laughing and playing. He walked in and announced that he could beat Michael Jordan in a one-on-one basketball game. Here's the funny part—he was serious. "No, I'm serious" he explained, as he began to tell us his strategy and plan to beat Mr. Jordan. Because of his abilities, creativity, and confidence, we are able to address him differently than his sister. He doesn't know yet, but he is destined to be a great planter. I watch his reactions of grandeur and fulfillment when his little brother wins a race or scores a touchdown, or his younger sister performs in a dance where he has taught her some of the moves. He brightens up and explodes with pleasure more than when he has experienced a victory of some sort of his own. He is a planter, and because of that, we painfully realize that we must allow him to be exposed to more of the elements without our help. It is a difficult thing for a planter to watch the stormy winds, scorching sun, and drenching rains batter his seedlings without trying to cover them or at least protect them from some of the elements. But it is a necessary part of the process, which makes the seeds strong enough to eventually survive on their own.

Our middle daughter is a precious soul. She was the baby for ten years until I met her mother and we married. This made her three of five instead of three of three in the household, and that was a rough adjustment for her. She is a gifted child with many talents, but in some arenas, she can be somewhat shy. She's an awesome dancer, singer, and actress; has outstanding computer skills; is able to solve some of the most difficult puzzles; her networking skills are second to none; and she has the *patience of Job* with small children. A surface inspection of her seed qualities might tell us to treat her as we did her older sister. However, three of five has a combination of things going on, and in order to be effective for her, there is a time to cuddle and nurture and create successful experiences, and there is a time to be blunt and display tough love to some of her choices. Therefore, to help her grow and mature, we as parents are very aware of the positive and negative qualities existing in her developmental process and at the drop of a hat switch into any mode necessary to help her continue to grow.

Our youngest son is probably the child who has experienced the most pain in our household. After the failure of my first marriage, when he was four years old, his mother called me to come get him. I'd just had my car repossessed and was living with another person, but I borrowed a car to pick him up. When I got there, his mother cracked the door open just enough for him to come out the door, dragging a trash bag behind him. I felt so badly for him, but at the same time, I was elated that he was coming to live with me. So we went to McDonald's and played in the balls and climbed through the tunnels until they told us we had to leave. To make a long story short, he's lived with me since then and has developed into a very influential young man. He's been forced to see all of my struggles, which is another story in itself. He is a caring person with great athletic ability and super problem-solving skills, and like his father, he has a very smooth swagger. But he can be the world's greatest procrastinator. I have watched him excel in everything that he has tried. His problem-solving skills, mathematics ability, and command of expressive language has opened many career paths to him.

If we chose to focus on his past experiences and the psychosocial issues that could have developed from those transitions, parenting him would have been no easy task. But since we understand that potential is what can be and we have taken the time to identify the type of seed that exists in him, we are able to address him with mostly principle-filled conversations and clear, specific, and concrete expectations that are always pointing toward increasing growth. He is destined for greatness, if and only if he would define that greatness for himself. This presents difficulty for the proud parent: "I want you to do this"; "I want you to do that"; "I think you are capable of"; "I know you can do it" are not statements that he can ever hear us say. His system of reasoning and problem-solving skills will kick in and he could possibly rebel with a sound plan of his own which points in the opposite direction. So in order to help this seed grow, we have to not only understand its type and characteristics, but we have to be active in removing any weeds that may be trying to choke him before he becomes a rooted plant producing seeds of his own. The baby boy is a thinker, and therefore his seed type is definitely a bean or corn.

Our youngest daughter, my baby girl, has always been the baby girl. However, when she was nineteen years old, she wanted to be anything but the baby girl. After my first marriage dissolved, her mother moved without my knowledge and I didn't see her for about four years. To make another long story short, due to the efforts of my awesome wife of today, we eventually got custody, and the baby girl has lived in our household since she was nine years old.

She is a gifted writer with all the emotions and imagination that come with that calling. She easily masters schoolwork and takes great pride in how she is viewed by her teachers and those who have authority over her. When she takes on tasks, she always strives to do her very best. However, when working cooperatively, she often becomes upset because others who may be working with her do not have the same level of commitment and self-established high standards. She is very sensitive about the feelings of others and consistently places consideration for them before her own needs and desires. She displays an introverted, bashful demeanor in most public settings, but when she feels comfortable, she knows how to work a room. She is probably the most intriguing of the five children raised in our household. Her work ethic, focus, and determination are second to none. She is easy to motivate and appreciative of little things, but she is easily misunderstood since she does not communicate her feelings readily. She does not like to make decisions. For example, when she was younger, when we took her to the mall to go shopping, it would take her so long to make decisions about what she wanted to buy, and sometimes, she walked away with nothing at all. When we took her to the grocery store and asked her which cereal she wanted to get, we would walk away from her to continue shopping while she decided, and she and her sister or brother would catch up with us two aisles later, usually with no boxes at all.

I believe she is a combination of a seed and a spore. She could survive in any setting and has many skills that are far superior to most around her. Some things happened in her early development, which called for us as parents to carefully prepare the soil around her to maximize her growth. The beautiful thing about being her planter is we get to watch her strengths take over once we make sure her spores or fragile tendencies take root and are strengthened. Once we cleared the path for her and she felt confident about the process, she quickly and readily owned the rest of the work and took pride in handling her own business. Thus, recognizing her combination of seed types has informed us and alerted us with ways to help support her growth.

We expect great things from all of our children. More importantly, we teach them to expect great things from themselves. The differences in each of them have trained us to recognize the differences in all seeds for which we prepare, water, or fertilize the ground. As parents, educators, or mentors, respecting the uniqueness of each of the seeds we are trying to grow is necessary. If we are not careful, we will provide too much of one thing and not enough of another, resulting in a devastating impact that could stunt the growth of the most precious thing we have been entrusted with—the seeds we mentor, educate, and parent.

## Cultural Awareness or Connection

Another area to consider when attempting separating types of seeds is culture. Although five basic concepts orbit when one examines the concept of culture—universal, ubiquitous, traditional, race-based, and pan-national—for purposes of this book, my focus on culture lies within the traditional realm. The traditional approach defines culture as country of domicile, including language, history, beliefs, and rituals. One is a member of a particular cultural group through birth, upbringing, and geographic location. Within a cultural group, one cannot ignore the impact that social class or gender may have on their rituals and beliefs. Cultural norms, values, perceptual sets, and so forth develop in response to environmental contingencies. I am proposing that the ideas of the dominant societal culture can no longer be that to which each seed is forced to assimilate. If you can't relate, you can't educate. It is simple as that!

As leaders of societal institutions, we often reinforce cultural meanings of behavior, thoughts, and feelings that are norms from our vantage point. A disadvantage of this approach is the possibility of diminishing the variances that exist within a single cultural group. Culture refers to the collection of ways of living that a group adopts to satisfy biological and psychological needs, including acceptable thoughts, behaviors, languages, and customs. In other words, each cultural subgroup creates and identifies with their own norms.

For the seeds in our urban arenas, the cultures of the home, the school, and the community remain at odds, presenting gaps in the consistency needed to help these seeds grow as they deserve to. In fact, many writers claim this rift between home, school, and community has been attributed in large measure to academic failure, high rates of suspension and expulsion, and the overrepresentation of black males, in particular, in special education programs and their underrepresentation in gifted education programs (Lewis 2010). However, I believe the rift between, home, school, and community is a major reason why the above factors exist in our urban arenas. In order to address the educational needs of urban students, educators must be open and willing to understand the central properties of urban culture to develop effective interventions that improve student achievement outcomes. Once again, in order to educate, you must be able to relate.

Pulling the weeds or disciplining is a part of cultivating and growing seedlings into fruit-bearing and productive plants. In order for parents and educators to help change inappropriate home or school behavior, an understanding of the logic that drives certain decisions in the existing and appropriate culture is imperative. Each geographical climate and seasonal cycle supports the growth of certain vegetation types. This is a reverse definition of the concept of the word *indigenous. Unless, we as planters understand the needs of the seeds, our well-intentioned interventions will not succeed.* Again, successful mentors, educators, and parents are those who are honest, open, and willing to equip themselves with information about the seeds' subculture and ethnic variations within their communication patterns. The insight gained by doing the work of "knowing the need of the seed" will enable strategic design of climates that will enhance and increase positive outcomes. Specific seeds have specific needs. Are you ready to adapt so you can meet them?

## Chapter Recap

Chapter 3        Specific Seeds Require Specific Needs
- Seed types and requirements
- My children and their differences
- Special education classifications
- Cultural awareness connections

## Chapter Questions

1. Briefly discuss the seed type of one of the youth you serve. Why do you feel that he or she is that type? How do you compensate your approaches to accommodate for that seed type?
2. Give three examples of how culture affects how you address seed types in your work?
3. What are your ideas on special education as they apply to its use in today's schools, and preparation for post-secondary education experiences?

# CHAPTER 4

# ACCEPT ONLY WHAT YOU EXPECT

## We Are Either Up or Getting Up

During the daily pursuit of purpose in the lives of every human being, two distinct phases of action are visible. Although these two phases may appear in many forms and contain various stages or concentrations within them, they are easily reduced to seeking or doing. Every human being on the planet is either in the midst of completing a task or is preparing to embark upon completing a task. One of the issues that arise from these two phases of action is the choice of tasks that we are seeking to accomplish.

Zig Ziglar, a famous motivational speaker, once said that there are always two things happening in his life—he was either up or getting up. He also maintains that in the pursuit of purpose, there are no secondary outcomes: either you achieve the goal or you don't. Mr. Ziglar has a plethora of work about the steps necessary to achieve goals, maintaining positive thinking, being proactive in preparation, resiliency, and application of principles to close the deal. I have listened to many of his lecturers and read a few of his books, and they seem to all wind up at the same conclusion: excuses result in stunting the growth of any seed you are trying to grow. I suggest that you listen to some of his work as he has been tremendously helpful to me. However, in order for the material printed by most of the authentic self-help facilitators to be productive in the average person's life, we must understand expectations. For the purposes of our discussion, we will simplify the world of expectations into two categories: reasonable expectations and high expectations.

## Approaches to Expectations

Internal Approach

The overarching theme of the word *expectation* can be divided into two approaches. The first approach is internal, meaning a person has a hope or a desire to become or achieve something. This sense of the word *expectation* is a powerful motivator. When a seed understands its potential, buys into its possible outcomes, and feeds off of a hope that is not seen and a desire to reach an expected ending, that seed becomes virtually unstoppable. Hope and desire are entities that no one can escape. If I were to move to the top of the tallest mountain and no human beings were in contact with me for a radius of five hundred miles, my hope and my desire would still be there with me. These ingredients are imprinted in our inner man and are not to be ignored.

However, realistically, our hope and our desires are affected by societal influences. Whether the influencing input is audiovisual, socioeconomic, or physiological, some factors of our environment have an influence on us. Therefore, as planters or sowers, we must be cognizant of the multiplicity of factors that affect the seeds we protect. We must strive to consciously address those factors that lower our ceilings and do the work to purify their effect on our internal expectations. We do not necessarily have the power to remove any of the influencing factors our seeds may encounter, but we can embrace them and use their momentum and influence as tools to assist the growth we are dedicated to accomplish in our seeds.

External Approach

The second approach to the word *expectation* has an external meaning. It encompasses the connotation that one is to live up to someone else's expectations or to be as good as someone else expects them to be. At first glance, most people would say that this version of the definition of *expectation* is negative and dangerous, and no one could quarrel with that conclusion. However, others may be of the school of thought that this extra motivation is needed to bring certain people up to par. The thinking behind this would entail that there were some developmental gaps that called for an external motivator to drive this group back on track toward an acceptable and productive pattern of thinking and decision-making.

Now that we know the intensity of an expectation is based on the strengths and weaknesses of its internal and external motivators, let us examine the degrees of an expectation and how they play in the lives of sowers and seeds. If I were to plant a handful of corn seeds, it would be reasonable to expect corn plants to grow. If I were to plant a handful of apple seed, it would be reasonable to expect apple trees to grow. Reasonable expectations are returns from a person or a thing that are not surprising; they are a given, they are supposed to be. Every rock, mineral, plant, and animal has its own chemical and physical composition that makes it uniqueness to everything else on the face of the planet. Every molecule is made up of elements that have specific configurations of protons, neutrons, and electrons. This molecular structuring leads to DNA fingerprinting that defines genetic tendencies as procreation progresses. In other words, the general purpose of everything on this planet is defined within its chemical and genetic makeup. Thus, there are some reasonable expectations on everything that exists on the face of this planet.

The seeds that we have metaphorically been referring to throughout this book are subject to the same principle. Every seed is meant to grow. If not, it would not be called a seed. A farmer does not marvel when he prepares his land, germinates his seeds, places them in the ground, and two weeks later a plant of the same kind of seed that he has planted appears. He would marvel if he planted one type of seed and a different type of plant sprung from the ground. Year in and year out, the farmer expects the soil, the seeds, chemicals of the atmosphere, the sun, and the rain to work together and yield a harvest of what he planted. As we spoke earlier, we cannot negate the preparation, planning, and care that the farmer invests to receive his harvest. However, it is not out of the question for us as mentors and educators to have reasonable expectations for the seeds that we are growing. But to do so, we must first identify the seed and its potential. In order for expectations to be calibrated correctly, they must align to the needs, potential, and purpose of the seeds. This means before we set any expectations on the seeds we parent, mentor, or educate, we have to thoroughly inspect those seeds to determine what is reasonable and what is beyond.

## Was NCLB a Good Thing for Urban Schools?

I know the No Child Left Behind (NCLB) system has been replaced with the Every Student Succeeds Act (ESSA). However, I think the NCLB system is a good example for us to be at peace with *accepting only what we expect* from the seeds we mentor, parent, or teach. Students graduating from colleges and universities in America have not been as competitive as some of the students who graduated from universities in other countries (Zhao, Kuh, and Carini 2005). NCLB was a response to that reality from our federal government. From their perspective, it showed that we are courageous enough to put resources where they need to be in an effort to correct a declining trend of academic performance and international competitiveness. As planters and sowers, we must follow that example displayed by our leaders, or at least most of it.

To me, the lesson we must extract from the NCLB act is that it is not unreasonable to expect every child to obtain mastery of the content prescribed in our public school system. It is not unreasonable to expect our seeds to assimilate to cultural influences and make informed decisions to become productive contributors in their communities. It is not unreasonable to expect our seeds to maintain a level of decorum and discipline that is within the norms of our society. It is not unreasonable to expect our seeds to take the information, nurture, and training that we have surrounded and saturated them with since the day they were born and pass that along to the next generation of seedlings.

However, it is unreasonable for us as planters to think that all of this can be achieved without first identifying the specific needs of the seeds for which we are responsible. Once that is accomplished, our next responsibility is to do the work to create conditions that are conducive for them to grow according to their needs, not our perceptions or conveniences. This is what the NCLB act did not account for. It irresponsibly overlooked the socioeconomic stressors that many urban and rural students battle on a daily basis and the cognitive and physical disabilities or challenges that our exceptional students live with and must overcome. The planter defines what is reasonable, but the seed determines how reasonability can be reached.

## Beyond Reasonable Expectations

Beyond reasonable expectations implies both high and unrealistic expectations. I conducted a study by visiting three urban public schools in three different states that were all performing low on their state's standardized assessments, and surveyed a sample of the teachers. They were asked to rate themselves on a 1-to-5 Likert Scale as it applied to this question: "Do you have high expectations for your students?" Of the 187 teachers surveyed, 97 percent gave themselves a score of a four or a five on the survey. As a result of that percentage, one may pose the question, "How can those teachers possibly have high expectations for their students when all of their schools were failing?" Don't the teachers know they are responsible for educating the students? It seems logical that an educator would rate himself low when the majority of students they are teaching are performing low on state standardized assessments.

Keep in mind that conclusion is based upon a different expectation, usually from people who are observing the educational system from the outside and do not understand the complexities of educating urban students, or students in general for that matter. Saying that these educators do not have high expectations is a generalizing statement that we should not make. Such overarching statements are unwise and unintelligent and they pass judgement on all educators.

Educators are people of abundance, meaning they always start a journey with the intention to give whatever they can to every human being that crosses their path. A true educator always believes that there's more than enough to go around. With this in mind, we cannot say that these educators do not have high expectations; but we can say that the ceiling of their expectations is defined by their own hope, vision, faith, and efficacy to move their students to a predetermined destination. Unfortunately, our society has silently defined that destination differently for the diverse groups of races, ethnicities, genders, and abilities that exist in our public schools.

## High Expectations

*High expectations are relative to the thinking of the person who is setting the expectations.* This is why it is necessary for organizations to have a mission statement and shared vision that define the expected outcomes of the work they do. As a school administrator, one of the greatest challenges I have ever faced has been getting educators who are not urban dwellers and do not seek to understand the culture to buy into a vision that encourages the same stimulating, intellectual atmosphere that exists in our suburban counterpart schools. I have detected an unconscious disbelief in the vast majority of the teachers whom I have led in our students from urban socioeconomically distressed neighborhoods. The actions I have witnessed have led me to believe that many educators are settled with an expectation that urban students cannot be trusted to govern themselves socially and master academia that would make them highly competitive in the post-secondary arena. Thus, a trade-off occurs. This unconscious and subtle hesitation is undetectable unless you are an urban dweller and accustomed to the consistently reinforced nonverbal systematic perpetuation of low expectations. Some of the subtleties that exist in our urban schools to which I am referring to are:

- a focus on discipline instead of instruction
- a *well-defined* discipline code of conduct but *broadly-defined* components of what an effective classroom or teacher should look like.
- regimented procedures and punishments that discourage congregation in common gathering points such as hallways, cafeterias, and auditoriums
- no structured system of integrated curriculum pacing, formative assessment mapping, or targeted personal intervention plans to increase academic mastery for struggling students.

Nonverbal subtleties are normal and acceptable occurrences in urban schools across the country. However, most teachers and administrators are clueless to the fact that they are unconsciously lowering their expectations by directing focus away from the potential of what the seeds could produce and toward nurturing the weeds that steal from and choke that potential. This is not to say these urban educators do not care about their students. As a matter of fact, I have witnessed with my own eyes that many of these educators care very deeply for the students that they instruct and come in contact with each day. Unfortunately, caring is a negligible quality and is simply not enough when it comes to establishing high expectations.

## A Master Teacher

As stated previously, I have come in contact with many educators who are not urban dwellers but are tremendously effective in the urban school system. For instance, Mrs. J is a teacher in an urban school district in the northeastern part of the United States. This young lady has taught in the same school district for over twenty years and has achieved positive results during her tenure. Although Mrs. J is not an urban dweller, she seeks to understand the culture and works hard not to judge, negatively or positively, any of the tragic scenarios and situations that many of her students have found to be a normal part of their lives.

As a former administrator serving in the school in which Mrs. J taught, I had the pleasurable opportunity to observe her classroom. Mrs. J exhibited all the qualities of a master teacher enabling her to receive exemplary marks on her summative observation forms. She was organized, neat, well-planned, and she established good rapport with her students and parents. Her students were always on task, her lesson's essential questions were clear and challenging, her classroom presence was commanding yet facilitating. Mrs. J was a master of creating teachable moments and stimulated intellectual conversation by always operating in higher cognitive questioning levels. She challenged her students to move beyond routine memorization and into the evaluation and synthesis arenas which stimulated students to create new ideas and thereby learn more.

As marvelous as Mrs. J is in real life and on the evaluation form, this is not how I know she has high expectations for her students. Mrs. J treats every student that walks through her classroom door the same. She greets them with a smile and a task, and neither of the two is optional. From day one, Mrs. J has made it clear to her students that she cares about them and what is going on in their lives, but she cares more about what they learn. She explains to them the opportunity that education brings and admits to her students that although not much can be done about their conditions today, it is her job to arm them with knowledge so they can make more informed choices which will make their tomorrow much brighter. Once she conveys that message and knows that it is understood, she begins to tirelessly meet the needs of each of her seeds to produce exemplary work.

As she reaches into her creative bag of tricks and facilitates the learning process of her students, she refuses to accept anything less than each student's personal best. Once her students reach a plateau of mastery that they have never achieved before, she praises them and pushes them to reach the next plateau after the one they just achieved. This is the process that proves Mrs. J has high expectations for her students. This process is rooted in a final plateau that is defined by a much broader and more influential world of literacy and not by what has traditionally been achieved in this particular urban community, school district, or school. Mrs. J has reached beyond those invisible but very real walls of status quo. With one hand, she has anchored her hope, belief, and faith in her students. With her other hand, she reaches to pull her students to the vision she has for them academically, socially, and developmentally.

Helping students reach higher may seem like a simple feat and something that all educators should be doing. I agree. However, the effective educator is divided into two distinct categories. The first category that describes an effective educator is a consciously competent master teacher, like Mrs. J, who deliberately utilizes methodologies to progress students academically and socially in an efficacious manner. The second category of an effective educator is what I have coined called not chosen. I named them called not chosen because they have an inherent gift to educate but they have not chosen to be committed to the work involved to become a master teacher. Unfortunately, the called not chosen educator is *unconsciously competent* and is more than likely relying on their instincts and inherent gifts and abilities with only a theory as to why they are effective. This is dangerous because unless they eventually encounter a master teacher or a skillful administrator, they could fall into the abyss of mediocrity that has, to their own unaware, gripped a large portion of our existing urban educators, thus neutralizing their super power to grow our seeds.

## Setting Expectations

In growing seeds, we should *accept only what we expect*. Setting expectations is not a negative thing to do for our seeds. In fact, if we don't set those expectations, our seeds can become confused and could lie dormant, thus aborting their purpose. If this occurs, the seeds then become potentially damaging to others and must be removed so the harvest can flourish as it was intended. It is our job to effectively, consistently, and most importantly continue to communicate a list of the reasonable expectations to all seeds in our care. This is synonymous to the farmer who inspects his fields daily, searching for incorrect patterns, poor irrigation, sun and shade issues, and pesticide and rodent control needs. Once the farmer sees those needs, he immediately acts upon them either himself or assigns someone in his the team to correct the problem. This is called clearing the field. As urban mentors, educators, and parents, we have a responsibility to clear the fields in the lives of the seeds we are growing. Creating environments that set the expectation that anything detrimental to the physical, social, emotional, and mental well-being of those seeds must be cleared. Setting this level of expectation creates a partnership between the seeds and the growers to maintain a culture of nurture and possibility.

## Clearing the Field

Often, a farmer surveys his field and recognizes holes in his crops where a bacteria or a parasite has begun to overtake his healthy plants, and could potentially destroy the whole crop. Keep in mind that the harvest the farmer gathers is his livelihood. Every ounce of his energy, all of his finances, his time, his family's provisions, and every resource is invested in an expected harvest. The stakes are high for the farmer and his family. By clearing the field and searching for any potential cancers that could destroy his ability to eat and survive the next year, the farmer teaches us to *accept only what we expect*. Often, to clear the field, the farmer will burn several acres of his crop to save the rest. I am not a farmer; however, I imagine that could be a painful experience after all of the work that has been invested. But the necessity of survival far outweighs any feelings involved in clearing the field.

The seeds that we as educators, parents, and mentors are responsible for cannot literally be burned, cut down, or ground up and turned into fertilizer for the next crop. Nevertheless, we do have to clear the field of poor attitudes, beliefs, behaviors, performance, and work ethic. It is our responsibility to not only set the level for reasonable expectations but also make sure they are carried out. We must *accept only what we expect*. If we don't take a strategic stand to accept only what we expect, then we will establish seeds that accept a culture of mediocrity or adopt and operate from what I call a welfare mentality. Those seeds will grow to expect handouts and have no intentions of relying upon their own potential or upon their own physiological design to produce a plenteous harvest. Many seeds fail to grow because we accept ill outcomes that we never expected.

## Chapter Recap

Chapter 4　Accept Only What You Expect
- Reasonable expectation
  - ○　Apple seeds yield apple trees

- Every seed is meant to grow
- Every human being is meant to learn
- High expectations
  - Every farmer expects their crop to feed them and produce more seeds
  - How do we know if we have high expectations for ourselves, for others
- Clearing the field
  - The farmer will destroy all molds, bacteria, and parasites
  - Poor performance, attitudes, and work ethic must go
- Seeking or doing
  - Are we seeking so they can be doing?
  - We are either up or getting up
  - Pursuit of purpose, no secondary outcomes

## Chapter Questions

1. Do you have high expectations? How do you know? Be specific.
2. What are the reasonable expectations for the seeds you are trying to grow?
3. Do you believe that society has defined the ceilings and floors differently for the diverse groups of students in our public schools? Why or why not?
4. In what ways does the structure of the organization in which you serve cause ceilings for urban seeds? In what ways does it remove them?
5. Discuss ways that you clear the field of things that can potentially damage the harvest?
6. List what you expect from your seed. Analyze your list and evaluate your action to determine if what you are expecting is what you are accepting.

# *Don't Be Afraid*
# *to Use Fertilizer*
# *and Pesticides*

## Don't Dumb It Down

I t is no secret that students in urban schools are up against some pretty difficult odds. They have to contend with a myriad of socioeconomic stressors like

- poverty
- dilapidated housing conditions
- unsanitary living arrangements
- unbalanced meals
- unsafe travel corridors
- low expectations
- lack of indigenous mentors and high-achieving examples
- stereotypical suggestions
- challenged self-images
- absence of the importance and parallel of education and its effect on real-world success
- family ties and loyalties that supersede aspirations
- intense negative peer pressure
- absent parents
- drug and alcohol influences
- ineffective educators
- crowded classrooms

And the list goes on.

It can be easy for educators, parents, and community stakeholders to "dumb down" efforts toward excellence for the average urban student. This common and grave mistake is often driven by compassion, as we are people too. We often look into the eyes of a student and see the weariness of their challenges. The compassion we feel for those students is warranted; but our actions must be calculated and strategic to best serve them so they can mature, grow, and produce a good harvest.

For instance, there have been times, as a school principal, that I have stretched the dress code, ignored the attendance policy, mediated away a suspension, or moved detention dates to accommodate students and parents. These acts could be construed as low expectations or weakness to the unenlightened observer. More accurately, they are wise strategies to keep students motivated and connected while simultaneously holding them accountable. It is a fact that every seed requires different needs, and in order to produce the best harvest, a farmer must carefully survey his crops and respond to growth and the lack thereof. The same goes for the seeds we are growing in our schools, homes, and communities.

We can no longer make excuses for poor work ethic linked to socioeconomic concerns, nor can we ignore issues that stunt the growth trajectory of the seeds we are growing. Society is too smart to be complacent with throwing up its hands and saying, "I don't know what to do!" We have too many studies, books, systems, and examples to continue to make excuses for slow or no growth from our seeds. From the operant behavior conditioning of B.F. Skinner, the instructional strategy work of Marzano, and the brilliance of Max Thompson's Learning Focused Model, just to name a few, we now know enough to make all seeds grow more efficiently. Accountability is a core issue in our urban schools, not only for students but for parents, community stakeholders, teachers, and most of all school administrators.

Although mediocrity is ultimately a choice, as mentors of urban youth, we are just as much to blame for the way the masses of these young people are settling for less than what they are capable of accomplishing. The quality of leadership is the single most impactful determinant that sets the boundaries for the choices of a group of people. "For they that lead this people cause them to err; and they that are led of them are destroyed" (Isaiah 9:16, ASV). This implies that more weight is on the shoulders of parents, educators, and mentors to find a different way to produce change than it is on the shoulders of the students to find that way themselves. A seed can only produce after its own kind. What our seeds are producing may not be a direct outcome of what we showed them, but it is a direct result of what we allowed to form and settle in the foundation of their character.

## What Weighs More

Although offensive and kind of gross, I want to project this visual to emphasize how important it is for us to have high expectations and discourage excuses at all times and by any means necessary for the seeds we are growing. A man was walking down the street and his dog pooped on his neighbor's lawn. Knowing that this neighbor becomes irate when this occurs, the man hurried to correct the situation before his neighbor noticed. The man quickly put a glove on and picked up the dog poop with his right hand. However, he was too late and his neighbor came outside loudly complaining, "How could you let your dog do such a thing? You should be watching that mutt more carefully!" Holding the dog poop partially behind his back but still visible in his right hand, the man held out his left hand and began gesturing it as he gave excuses to why he wasn't watching his dog. Focusing on the man's hands, the neighbor promptly responded, "Excuses, that's all you ever give, excuses. Don't you know they are just empty words? At least your other hand is *full* of crap." The moral of the story is that excuses aren't worth crap! Although undesirable, at least the dog mess is a tangible thing. In every case, and on every scale, the dog poop will outweigh the excuse.

The dog poop is a result of a physical action; it is a reaction to a need or an urge. With a little patience, the dog can be trained to relieve itself in a desired location where the ground can be used as a compost mixture which creates fertilizer that will help bring life to many seeds. On the other hand, the excuse is empty and idle and yields no return on investment. Yet we have studied to eloquently present them, seemingly afraid to admit that we have to change or enhance what is feeding the seeds we are growing. Seeds gain their nutrients from the soil, and the only way to change the composition of that soil so those seeds maximize their growth is to add fertilizer. There are also other risks to the seeds once they begin grow. To protect young seedlings from any parasites that might feed on their brilliance and cause a hindrance to their growth, a good pesticide must be applied. Don't be afraid to use fertilizer and insecticides if needed to protect and help flourish the seeds we are growing.

## Fertilizer for the Soil

Fertilizer is a substance added to soil with the purpose of increasing or replacing the nutrients depleted by plant growth and weatherization. The key ingredients in fertilizer are nitrogen, phosphorus, and potassium; these are known as the macronutrients of the soil (i.e. values, character, and beliefs). However, there are other nutrients that fertilizers add to the soil in smaller amounts. They are called micronutrients (i.e. education, goals, relationships).

Staying consistent with the metaphor of this book, it follows that our urban children have a plethora of nutrient deficiencies in the foundational soil of their lives that have a negative effect on the fertility of their harvest. As educators, mentors, and parents, we have the responsibility to ensure that the macronutrients needed to facilitate maximum growth are always present in the lives of the seeds we nurture. This is a full-time job. It is imperative that we, as effective mentors, parents, and educators, supplement the soil of the seeds we serve with sound guidance, disciplined goals, supportive encouragement, and windows to dream through. This cannot be done without getting our hands dirty. We cannot be afraid to get into the inner circles of our seed's cultural existences. Once we do so, we can identify what macronutrients need supplementing and provide them to the best of our ability. Since this is our responsibility, we must foster relationships that allow us to cross the boundaries that are presently preventing us from talking openly with young people and their families about things that can be done to better fertilize the harvest that each seed can produce.

Remember, the purpose of this book is not to illuminate explicit strategies but to stimulate thinking around principles so mentors, educators, and parents can have a deliberate direction while preparing and nurturing growth in the seedlings they serve. Please do not misunderstand my position about books that highlight explicit strategies and instructional models. I believe they are necessary and tremendously informative and helpful. However, many times have I witnessed the acquisition of the best equipment that money could buy but with little or no knowledge about the true capabilities of the equipment and how to apply it in the situation for which it was purchased. The outcome of those situations has always reduced a magnificent product into producing a mediocre outcome. I believe we are at a point in the social and cultural development of our public schools that is telling us to step back and look at our approach to the task at hand. The Every Student Succeeds Act (ESSA) has established the need for accountability; now we must become more thoughtful in our planning and take time to focus on culture and those who are establishing the culture.

As we seek to understand existing cultures before being understood, and identify elements that may be missing or lacking, we will naturally try to fill those gaps to facilitate proper growth and provide a healthy foundation from which to grow. This is the process of applying fertilizer. Although different for every child we mentor, teach, or parent, its principle, purpose, and procedure remains consistent—seek to understand things from the perspective of the seed and then proceed to employ interventions that address their needs and point them in the most constructive direction possible.

Often, there are times when the foundational soil is already fine and conducive to nurture young seedlings but there is something foreign stunting the growth of the harvest. Often, a pest of some sort enters into the picture and begins to cause damage in the lives of our seedlings. Again, we must first identify the pest before we can create a game plan to eliminate it. This will require communication and relationship. These are both bidirectional processes and can only happen in a nonjudgmental climate that encourages give and take. Once the pest is identified, the proper pesticide must be applied. The first step in applying a pesticide is the act of exposing the damage the targeted pest has caused by directing attention to a plant that has been mutilated, chewed on, and starved by the pest.

One way of doing so could be to have guest speakers, who have chosen to ignore their education or were involved in criminal activity and jailed, share with the seedlings their firsthand experiences of the outcomes of negative choices. Another method is to build a direct connection to the seedlings you are growing and the pests indigenous to the cultures in which those seedlings exist. For example, educators and parents could illuminate the damage drugs and alcohol have done to the community by working together to have young people do surveys and read case studies and statistical reports about the effects those things have had on the community in social studies classes or science classes. They can share their findings by creating presentations in which they involve their parents or mentors to deliver to their classrooms in front of their peers and teachers.

## Pesticides to Exterminate the Pests

A pesticide is any substance or mixture of substances intended for preventing, destroying, or repelling any pest. For our purposes, a pest is anything that destroys property, spreads disease, and is a harmful nuisance that stunts growth or aborts a person's original pursuit of purpose. Obviously, we cannot be afraid to identify the pest, call it by name, and educate ourselves and the all stakeholders concerned. Once identified, it must be attacked with a pesticide designed to eradicate its negative effects on our seedlings. However, this will call for a paradigm shift in thinking. We must do the opposite of the popular "see no evil, hear no evil" attitude. Instead, we should work together to get involved, discuss and derive plans to expose the pests, and openly apply pesticides to those things we now treat as taboo and impolite. We have the power to chase away every pest that hinders the progress of our seed. To accomplish this task, a degree of courage will be required for two reasons: (1) most pests are creepy, gross, and unpleasant things that we do not want to touch, look upon, or talk about; (2) some of the pests in the lives of our seedlings exist because of things we failed to clean up, address, or are presently doing ourselves.

Thus, it takes courageous individuals to apply pesticides in the lives of our seeds. Keep in mind that the presence of such strength is not the absence of fear. Dealing with abuse, addiction, self-centeredness, racism, delinquency, perceived lack of motivation, poor self-images, and poverty mind-sets is not easy to do and often stirs up *F*alse *E*motions that *A*ppear *R*eal (FEAR). When applying pesticides, we must embrace the uneasy feeling that accompanies the task.

Keep in mind that the pest is not only a nuisance to us as sowers; it is a bother to the seedlings as well. However, we have to show our seeds that they do not have to succumb to the pest. We should demonstrate authority over it by addressing it head on, not allowing it to fester and become a mysterious thing that dictates our progress by FEAR. Not only is this a very difficult thing to do, depending upon your level of self-actualization, this is probably the most important thing you can do for your urban seed. Applying fertilizer and pesticides requires action, and it is this type of courageous and honest modeling that brings hope and motivation to our seed. In short, don't be afraid to use fertilizer and pesticides. The lives of your seeds depends upon your ability to do so.

## Chapter Recap

Chapter 5    Don't Be Afraid to Use Fertilizer and Pesticides
- A big mistake is to make excuses for poor ethics
  - Address issues head on
  - Provide supports for high expectations
- What to look for while doing inspections
  - The purpose of fertilizers
    - Types of fertilizers
    - Uses of fertilizers
  - Purpose of insecticides
    - Types of insecticides
    - Uses of insecticides
- We must create a balance between the existing culture and a new way of thinking

## Chapter Questions

1. Choose one stressor and discuss ways you can help seeds overcome the effects of it without negating its existence or compromising your mission.
2. Explain how the process of accountability acts as a fertilizer or a pesticide in the lives of the seeds you are growing?

3.  How important do you think it is to push into the cultural realities of seeds to be able to apply the proper fertilizer? Why?
4.  What does the analogy of applying fertilizer to the lives of our seeds mean to you?
5.  Talk about a time you have applied pesticides to help your seeds grow. Was it easy to do or difficult?
6.  List some of the obvious pests to the growth of our seeds, and outline how can we face those pests head on?

# CHAPTER 6

# *Believe It or Not, the Seedling Is Trying to Grow*

## I Beg to Differ

T he dropout rates from public schools across the nation have declined from 10.9 percent in 2000 to 5.9 percent in 2015 (NCES 2017). This translates to two and a half million seeds who, for one reason or another, choose to walk away from their high school education without completing it (NCES 2017). Approximately, 88 percent of those two and half million seeds live in an urban or rural demographic (NCES 2017).

Achieve is a national a nonprofit organization created by a group of governors whose mission is to lead the effort to make college and career readiness a priority across the country so that students graduating from high school are academically prepared for postsecondary success. According to the research Achieve has published, there are an estimated two thousand failing high schools, sometimes called "dropout factories," that are responsible for a disproportionate number of students who reach adulthood unequipped for college or careers (Achieve 2009). Unfortunately, this is not a phenomenon exclusive to high schools. There are thousands of chronically low-performing elementary and middle schools that are part of the problem as well since these schools feed low-performing high schools (Achieve 2009). Although college enrollment is increasing for urban, minority, low-income, and high-poverty students, the completion rate from those postsecondary institutions is tremendously low (NRC Research Center, 2016).

Percent of at-risk students enrolling and completing postsecondary programs in six years.

|  | High Poverty | Low Income | High Minority | Urban |
|---|---|---|---|---|
| Enrolling in postsecondary programs | 51% | 54% | 57% | 62% |

| Completing postsecondary program (six years later) | 18% | 24% | 28% | 28% |
|---|---|---|---|---|

According to Greene and Winters (2006), many urban settings across the country share similar statistics that are the symptoms of a greater disease suggesting the existence of multigenerational devaluing of school engagement. The lives of the seedlings in urban areas are often filled with very challenging responsibilities, so they mistakenly tend to place the commitment to school lower on their priority ladder because it is not considered a necessity for immediate survival.

Often, seeds do not see the relevance and connection of their assignments in school to their daily lives. Additionally, as a result of repeated cycles of teen pregnancy, the generational age gap between urban youth and their parents is typically less than three quarters of what is traditionally a generation's age span—twenty years. This perpetuated cycle leads to the rejection of school by parents and children as their thinking is overlapped by the proximity of their ages and developmental stages (McDermott and Rothenburg 2009). If a parent had a bad experience in school, they assume their child's experience is going to be a bad one as well. Tragically, they model a judgmental and unsupportive example that undermines the need to trust the ability that education possesses to create opportunities in one's life. Unfortunately, this cycle is likely to continue and become prevalent in third and fourth generations as these perceptions are shared with yet another cohort of children (University of Chicago 2012).

Given these daunting truths, it is easy for educators, parents, and mentors to conclude that our seeds do not want to grow. I beg to differ! I believe that the norms of our urban cultures have conditioned our seeds to settle for destinies far below their actual potentials. In order to know what our seeds are actually thinking, we have to ask them and include them in factfinding and data collection processes.

This chapter presents actual comments students have presented when interviewed concerning their feelings about the educational experience at their local school. In my career, I have had the opportunity to travel to different states and serve as a consultant to educational institutions in several urban centers. When I travel from site to site, I take the opportunity to interview students in a focus group style. I always ask a question that basically seeks to know why they keep coming back to the particular school which they are attending. Below, I have included three tables that share data I collected from three different urban schools in which I had the privilege to consult from 2010 to 2012. All three of the schools represented below are in highly urban communities, serve students who have at some point dropped out of school and returned to finish, or who are at risk of dropping out and chose to attend a special program to get the extra support they need to complete their high school diploma.

## What Do Our Seeds Have to Say

The tables are divided into two columns: + and Δ. The + column lists the comments the students shared concerning the things they like about the school and wish were a part of the culture of the schools they attended prior to attending this one. The Δ column lists the things students would change in the school they are now attending. Keep in mind, these schools are designed specifically to address the academic and social needs of at-risk students. Thus, it is not surprising that a long list of change requests was collected from the students participating in the interview. In each of the three schools, a strong student advisory council exists and is active in the life of the school. When interviewed as a group, the students were asked two questions: (1) What things are different about this school and the ones you attended before? (2) If there was something about this school you would change, what would it be?

Their responses were as follows:

Table 1. School A's Responses to "Why" Survey

| + | Δ |
|---|---|
| Staff work with students because of smaller classes to atmosphere is more personal. We feel like it belongs to us. | We need to find a way to integrate the new students into the life of the school without so much distraction after mental toughness. |
| Focus on attendance. They call you, they find out what is going on with you, care about the trouble you might have at home, and they always take you back. | |
| They teach you to look past your diploma to your future after Youth Build then give you steps to focus on what's next. | |
| Stay with you after you get your diploma. (This program is about life.) | |
| Teach life skills like leadership, workforce readiness, how to interact, communication skills, and money management. | |
| They listen to us. They own our problems along with us. | |
| Create a community atmosphere where we all help each other. It is a safe place to belong. | |

| | |
|---|---|
| They reward our accomplishments and help us feel proud and positive about ourselves. | |
| Staff members keep us focused on timelines and encourage us not to procrastinate. We see things happening in our lives. | |
| They provide positive counseling for the issues we face every day like drugs and physical abuse. | |

Table 2. School B's Responses to "Why" Survey

| + | Δ |
|---|---|
| The school is a comfort zone with good relationships like a family. | Some students are not willing to change. |
| Smaller classes with less drama so you can learn more. | |
| Academics are more focused toward making you learn and go to college. | |
| They give you a second chance and help you realize the importance of education. | |
| We learn about our history and get pride in our heritage. | |
| There is no judgment of each other. It's easy to be yourself. | |
| There is good technology, and we use it create real things we need to learn. | |

| | |
|---|---|
| We have strong support system and wake up calls. They find ways to help you in school and out of school. They own your problems with you until it is all over. | |

Table 3. School C's Responses to "Why" Survey

| + | Δ |
|---|---|
| It is a safe environment where teachers and students push you to do better. | We wish there were flexible hours for those of us coming from a long distance. |
| There is plenty of schoolwork to help you focus on goals and not the streets. | We would like to start a debate club. |
| You get hope from here. They help you believe that you can go on to college and other dreams you may have. | |
| They support you and keep you informed of your status in enough time that you can do something about it. | |
| The teachers understand our problems. They have seen it all before and know how to help us. | |
| There are plenty of afterschool activities to keep us out of trouble. | |
| We are a family. | |

| | |
|---|---|
| We always talk about our future. We use words like *hope* and encourage each other to go to college and help others to get there as well. | |
| They care. | |

After analyzing and coding the data captured from the interviews, five common themes and four common topics emerge.

Five Common Themes and Topics Captured from Focus Group Interviews

| Common Themes | Common Topics |
|---|---|
| 1. Educators care about the academic progress of their students. | care |
| 2. Educators care about the life issues students face outside of the school house walls. | care |
| 3. The school has created a safe family-like atmosphere where each person is responsible for the other. | community |
| 4. The major focus of the school is to prepare students to access their future. | accountability |
| 5. Educators are comfortable talking about, addressing, and offering solutions to issues indigenous to urban communities. | action |

Nothing on these lists is surprising. In fact, they are answers similar to what I would have given if I had been asked the same questions. Perhaps these responses are similar to how you would respond as well. Our seeds are crying out to us, pleading for us, to give them the things we already know they need. As I stated earlier, this is not a book of strategies; it is a book of approaches, thought processes, attitudes, and foundations that allow us as mentors, educators, and parents to better nurture the seeds we are growing to increase the probability for them to produce more plenteous harvests. We must listen to our seeds and hear their requests because, believe it or not, the seeds are trying to grow.

## Things I've Seen

To reinforce the conclusions found when interviewing students across the country, I decided to research some peer-reviewed articles and studies to see if there were any similarities. Have you ever felt like you've done something right but felt the need to make sure you were on point? Well, lo and behold, consistencies and confirmations were jumping out at me in every study I read. Man, that felt good! However, there was one article that really touched me as I read it—"Seeing the Pedagogies, Practices, and Programs Urban Students Want" by Kristien Zenkov of George Mason University. Although it is a little dated, if you are interested in mentoring urban youth, I suggest you find and read her study in its entirety. Reflecting upon the privileged career I've had and opportunities to serve the youth with whom I have crossed paths, I noticed some similarities within the text of the Zenkov paper and scenarios I have experienced along the way. I thought it would be fun to share a few of those stories with you followed by a conclusion from Zenkov's work.

## A Poet and I Didn't Know It

I once had a student who was known to be very mouthy. She was a petite young lady full of energy and opinions. Her goal was to be a lawyer, and as a result, she felt it was her duty to argue every chance she got. Although she was very intelligent and scored high on standardized tests, her grades were low because she could not stay in class long enough to receive new assignments and excel on them. One day, I noticed her writing in a journal at lunch. We were planning a talent show around Character Education, and I felt she may want to participate. I approached her and asked if she would share some of her poetry, a spoken word, or a rap in the show, and her eyes lit up. A few days later, she came to me with a rhythmic poem that told the story of her father's death and the daily struggle her family faces to rebuild. I was floored! I pride myself on knowing my students and I didn't know of this tragedy. Instantly, I understood the young lady much better and I saw that she was crying for help.

We educators were the only ones in position within her life that were consistent and stable enough to give it to her. She and I began to talk about the piece she wanted to perform, and from that discussion, I learned that the reason she was missing so much school was that she was helping with her family. Nearly her whole immediate family was suffering with depression and she was angry with everything around her because she felt as if life was playing a cruel joke on her. When I asked what the school could have done differently to support her, she stated that she simply wanted her teachers to be more aware that these issues happen more often than they know to people in urban communities. She went on to say that she wished her teachers would try to understand what she was feeling because that might help relieve some of the pain and pressure she was enduring. Most importantly, she was hoping that someone would tell her what to do and offer solutions to help her stay current with her assignments and in-school responsibilities because she has goals too and has every intention of reaching them. To map this story to the four common topics in the charts above, this student is simply asking the school to *care* and *take action* to help her complete her education successfully.

## I Assumed He Was All Right

On another occasion, a teenage young man attended a school in which I served as an administrator. He was very introverted and often seemed distracted and guarded. He didn't follow along with the crowd, nor did he get in trouble. His grades and standardized scores were in the proficient and advanced range. To most of us, this young man had a bright future and was a model student. In our weekly meetings, the guidance counselor began expressing some concerns about this student, and I carelessly dismissed her inquiries. Until one day, she brought him into my office and shut the door. She told him to tell me what he had said to her. He said, "I feel so alone, like there is no one to help me be good at anything."

I happened to know this young man lived with his mother who was singlehandedly raising him while his father was living in another state and not involved with his son at all. I also knew he could run very fast because I often went outside and raced with the students to encourage them to play sports and stay active. Understanding that he simply craved the attention of a father figure, we talked for a while until he seemed at ease and I immediately connected him with a local church that had a strong young men's mentoring program. In fact, one of the men came to the school that day to meet the young man and invited him to "hang with his crew," as he put it. He was paired with a mentor who has been a great inspiration and positive impact in his life by spending time with him and encouraging him to pursue his dreams and aspirations. The intervention in this scenario maps to the *caring* and *community* common topics found in the charts above.

According to Zenkov, this is the conclusion one can draw from the experiences of these two students

> Youth look to teachers to model the caring, but still professional, adult/youth relationships they often do not find outside of school. Teachers' pedagogies might rely more intentionally on these relationships and on counseling youth about the nature of these supportive connections. Schools might better connect to mentoring programs and the school curriculum might include life skills classes that help youth deal in healthy ways with the daily pressures that they are facing. (Zenkov 2009)

## For My Little Sister

I recall a young lady who had become pregnant and dropped out of school as she chose not to withstand the pressure of the streets, her boyfriend, and her family. I remember talking to her right before she withdrew. She spoke of the pain her parents caused when they told her she had to leave the home because she became pregnant and how her focus was now on doing what was right for her baby. Despite my best efforts to help her realize that education will bring greater opportunities so she could better provide for her child, she gave me a hug, and with tears in both of our eyes, she signed out of school at seventeen years old with no intention to return. The only thing I could do was watch her walk away and pray that God would shield her from unnecessary storms in her life.

Two years later, I was working at a different school in the same city and the same young lady came in to enroll and finish her high school diploma. I was so happy to see her that I picked her up and swung her around right in the middle of the office. After she got her enrollment package and finished talking to the case managers, she came and talked with me. I couldn't wait to ask her, "What changed your mind? Why are you returning to school?" She told me that her little sister got pregnant as well and her parents were making her sister leave the home as they had done with her.

Her little sister came to her for a place to live and was talking about quitting school as well. The young lady pleaded with her little sister to remain in school and she promised to return to school herself so they could finish together. She went on to tell how excited she was and afraid at the same time. But most of all, she was honored and determined to be a good role model because she cares about her sister's future. This scenario maps to three of the four common topics in the charts above—*caring*, *accountability*, and *take action*—as the young lady stepped up to the plate to save her little sister.

According to Zenkov (2009) the conclusion drawn from this young lady's experience was that

Adolescents serve as family and community cornerstones: They see themselves as mentors for the young people in their lives, models for peers, and potential subjects of mentoring they still hope the adults in their lives might provide.

[This young lady's] efforts suggested that teachers and schools should provide structures to appeal to and support these mentoring roles if we want adolescents to engage with school. Such structures might include credit bearing real world service learning or internship experiences tied to the mentoring activities with which young adults are involved. (Zenkov 2009)

## He Still Has a Chance

This story occurred early in my teaching career during the 1990s. There was a young man who lived with his father and his grandfather. His grandfather was very militant, and because of his experience with other races, he believed in racial separatism. He felt the system was against all black folks and that we should in no way buy into the propaganda that they should trust the US government. The young man's father was a local drug dealer who had a lot of street clout and was very well-known in the community for his control and protection of the three- or four-square blocks of territory in which he conducted his business.

About two weeks before Christmas, the student's father was arrested and held without bail for drug trafficking and homicide. My student was devastated! He loved his father and was not very close to his grandfather, his mother had died several years earlier, and he was now a target in the community based on the life that his father had lived. He was a senior in high school and was a half decent math student, so we convinced him to take the Armed Services Vocational Aptitude Battery (ASVAB) exam. He did very well and wanted to join the Marine Corps, but his Grandfather forbade it. After many phone conversations (that could be categorized as arguments), I visited the grandfather and shared my upbringing with him. I talked about my time in the marines and the perspective I gained from the experience. I was honest that I did not agree with everything that I was told, but I had a strong father (about the same age as the grandfather) who had taught me to always think for myself and set me on a path to help others grow and become somebody influential.

In a very humble way, I suggested that it was time for him to do the same for his grandson. After some deliberation, he conceded and the young man joined the Marin Corps. We kept in touch for about ten years as his career flourished and his rank continued to climb. The last time I spoke with the young man, he had gone to Officer's Candidate School (OCS) and was serving in his third enlistment as a captain in the US Marine Corps, intending on serving a full twenty-year career. By stepping outside the walls of the school house, I believe we saved that young man's life. Of the four common topics listed in the tables above, this scenario maps to the *action* and *community* categories.

According to Zenkov (2009), the conclusion drawn from this young man's experience was that

> Not all adults in the lives of our urban youth are positive influence and we should not assume that they are. If we want the adults in [student's] lives to serve as models, we might have to train them how to do so. All urban teachers might be required to serve as adult educators, working not just with the youth who show up in their classrooms, but also in formal ways with the adults in these adolescents' lives. (Zenkov 2009)

## Mistake to Mentor

This young man was not a student of mine but was an active parent who owns a construction company and volunteers tirelessly at his daughter's middle school where I happened to be an administrator. This young man had a rough life and was labeled a trouble maker and a delinquent by the adults in the schools he attended. He made a terrible mistake in his past and as a result was sentenced to five years at the state penitentiary. After serving his time, it was hard to find a job to help provide for his daughter who was then five years old. But he persevered and continued to fight to stay on the right path.

Seven years later, he comes to the same school where teachers had labeled him a menace to society and gives his time, his talent, and his money to help avert poor choices and lost chances in the lives of the young people presently attending that school. He simply does not want his daughter and her friends to make the mistakes he has made, so he has decided to get involved. This scenario maps to all four common topics in the charts above: *caring, community, account- ability*, and *action*.

The conclusion drawn from this young man's experience was that

> We might expand our definition of poten- tial mentors to include even students who have not had academic success or who have been posi- tioned as disruptive school influences. The power of change and connection that fallen students bring to the table is more powerful than we can predict. I believe this young man's daughter will not end up in the same situation as her father, simply because of his impartation of wisdom and transparency. (Zenkov 2009)

## Can't Ask What You Don't Know

This young lady came into my office with tears streaming down her face, holding a college application in her hand and frantically asking for help. She wanted to go to college and was clueless about what steps to take to get there. She was a senior, and it was near the end of March when she approached me. I felt so badly that we as a system had not better informed our students of the college entrance procedure that I stopped what I was doing to hear what she had to say. She was upset that she didn't know what to do to apply to college. She clearly wanted to go to college but had little support from home, not because they didn't care or want her to pursue a college education but because she would be a first-generation student and she nor her family had any idea what Free Application for Federal Student Aid (FAFSA), Scholastic Aptitude Test (SAT), American College Testing (ACT), application fee, or admissions office was. Part of me wondered how she got this far in high school without being familiar with any of these terms. However, we had to start from where we were if college was going to be an option at all. The more we talked and the further we got into the process, she began to ask pointed questions.

One day when I was talking to her mother on the phone telling her why she needs to provide a copy of her tax return and sign the FAFSA application, my student began sharing her feelings out loud to me. Since she became emotional, I hung up with her mother and let her vent. Essentially, she was becoming aware that we as a system had failed to make sure she was educated about all her options. Surprisingly, she was not as angry at us as she was at herself. I explained that she couldn't ask questions that she didn't know and tried to get her to focus forward and not backward. I believe she did just that; however, it seemed as if her determination was then coming from a perspective of proving herself worthy to those she felt had failed her.

I believe her need to prove to others that she can succeed has become a response to a culture of judgmental conclusions that have the radioactive fallout of low expectation. We persisted, and the young lady went on to graduate from one of the nation's oldest Historically Black Colleges and Universities (HBCU), Lincoln University. This scenario maps to three of the common topics found in the charts above: *caring, action,* and *accountability.*

According to Zenkov (2009), the conclusion drawn from this young lady's metaphor was that

> Many students expressed anger toward teachers and school structures that seemed to indict youth for the difficulties they were encountering. City youth feel like they get only one opportunity to succeed—in school and life— and they interpret teachers' actions as deeming

them bound for failure. Even the seemingly obvious practice of asking teachers to identify one strength they observed in each student—as often as once per week—might help youth to recognize the hope they should be finding in their schools. (Zenkov 2009)

## We Are in This for the Long Run

This young lady was caught with a young man in the school in a compromising sexual predicament early in October. I want to focus on the young lady for the purpose of this example. However, I do not want anyone to think there was not an elaborate process in delivering consequences to the male student as well, because there was. We went through all of the standard operating procedures in helping a young person who is making those types of poor choices. Happily, we began to see a very positive change in the young lady. Her grades and test scores began to increase, her attendance was high, there were no disciplinary referrals pointed at her, and she was involved in the life of the school. She completed the school year with accolades and was promoted to the next grade. The next school year started off strong, and we believed she was on the right track was assigned to be one of the student ambassadors for the whole building.

Suddenly, all her positivity came to a screeching halt. She began to get involved in fights, missing school, being asked to leave classes, and her grades and scores were plummeting. We, the instructional team, scratched our head and wondered what happened. I was at a basketball game at a local gym; I saw the young lady and went to ask her how things were going. When I approached her and gave my customary a hug, she shamefully looked down and wasn't as friendly as she usually was toward me. I told her she was one of my favorites and I was on her side no matter what. Before I could say anything else, she began to tell me how she had made a mistake and doesn't know how to get out of loop she has herself in.

She referred back to being caught in the school in that compromising sexual predicament. It turned out she was doing that to stay close to a young man who was selling weed. She explained how grateful she was for the interventions we put in place to help her and that her biggest lesson was that she realized she didn't have to follow in the footsteps of others who have gone before her. She felt as if she was worth more. "Everything was good, until I made that mistake," she said.

Apparently, she had relapsed and self-medicated one night and an unwise sexual act occurred. Since then, she has been carrying guilt and shame. By not forgiving herself and moving on from that single act, she has been caught in a loop of self-destruction. Because of her previous failure, she was unwilling to engage in school for fear of not meeting the expectations of the adults who had stood behind her before. She clearly didn't understand our dedication to her was for the long run. We understood that she would need to lean on us several times before she could totally embrace the opportunities education was presenting for her to change her quality of life, and thus her children's lives, and her children's, children's lives.

I did my best to encourage her to come back to school so we would get her involved with some of the afterschool programs to fill her time with positive and caring adults. I shared that we all make mistakes and no one was judging her, but she owes it to herself to learn from the mistake and press forward. This scenario maps to all four of the common topics found in the charts above, *caring, action, community* and *accountability*.

According to Zenkov (2009), the conclusion drawn from this young lady's sharing was that

> Urban adolescents can give up on themselves easily, and they often feel that teachers and family members abandon them even more quickly. Teachers and schools might take risks to provide youth with chances to succeed—day after day, through what might seem like elementary strategies—to focus on devising solutions to the challenges of their peers, families, and communities. (Zenkov 2009)

The lesson these scenarios should be communicating is that we as mentors, educators, and parents must look past the barren conditions of the fields in which our seeds exist. We must not only envision plenteous and abundant crops as a harvest, we must also constantly tell ourselves that the purpose of a seed is to grow and it wants to fulfill that DNA-defined task that exists within. If we believe that the seed wants to grow, it becomes easier to do the extra things to clear the field and provide the jumpstart or restart that our urban seeds require. Take it from me as a parent, mentor, and teacher of urban youth; it won't take long before it becomes clear that those extra efforts are good investments that will yield a great return. We must believe the seeds are trying to grow!

## Chapter Recap

Chapter 6    Believe It or Not, the Seeds Are Trying to Grow
- The state of urban education
  - Poor graduation rates
  - Plethora of socioeconomic stressors
- Student leadership council interviews
  - Students tell why they keep coming back to school
- Zenkov research mapped to true scenarios
  - More student attitudes about school as it applies to their lives

## Chapter Questions

1. If multigenerational devaluing of school engagement plagues our seeds, how can we break that cycle? Or is it possible to break at all?
2. Are all five common themes and four common topics mentioned in this chapter necessary to create a nurturing school environment? Elaborate.
3. In your opinion, which of the students in the Zenkov study best confirms the message that seeds are trying to grow? Which least confirms the message?

# CHAPTER 7

## EVEN THE PLANTER NEEDS CULTIVATING

## Definition of Cultivation

The word *cultivate* is quite fascinating. It defines a specific task as well as a process of an idea. The most popular definition of the word is "to prepare land or soil for planting with the intention to reap a maximum harvest" (*Newberry House Dictionary* 2016). This suggests that we must deposit some sort of work or investment in a thing in order to get a return. Cultivation is a deliberate act that expects to reap a harvest. Thus, as parents, educators, and mentors, we should prepare with purpose. Our actions should be deliberate and with an intention that causes our seeds to grow as developmentally consistent as possible.

To cultivate is also used in the context of developing and refining an understanding of an idea such as art, music, human behavior, child development, and so on. Aligning with the prior meaning of *cultivation*, this definition requires the investment of formal study of a topic. When I say *formal*, I am not limiting this process only to schools and universities. Studying is an action that requires submitting to what is necessary to learn more about a desired topic. The act of studying could include practicing, reading, examining, listening, or analyzing. This work is an external act that produces an internal result that causes a change within the studier that cannot be reversed. Although it is widely accepted that this meaning of the word *cultivate* is a requirement of a master teacher to be effective, it is often overlooked that parents and mentors indulge in this work just as intently.

The only difference between the educator group and the parent/mentor group is apparent in the third part of the definition of *cultivate*, which is to court and pursue. Educators are required to be responsible for their own professional development (PD). Most public school districts have built in some system of PD to insure all educators are at least introduced to the latest research and best practices. I say "at least introduced to" because many educators and the systems in which they work do not see the value in PD. Although this is probably a result of the existence of management-centered and not leadership-centered administrators, professional development is the opportunity for educators to court their gift and pursue the perfection of effective and productive instructional delivery. Parents and mentors can take classes, read books, and attend sessions to do the same; but professional development or expanding expertise in some manner is an unavoidable requirement to be an effective educator, mentor, or parent. Thus, we conclude that even the sower or planter needs cultivating.

We must first allow ourselves to be cultivated so we can support the seeds we are trying to grow. The principle of reciprocity is in play when we are growing the next generation. Those young people will produce a harvest that is directly proportionate to the amount of cultivation to which they are subjected. This is why it is important to create a culture of cultivation in ourselves as parents, mentors, and educators. The more we know, the further they go.

## Cultivation Is a Way of Life

My father was eighty-five years old when he did something that was truly life changing for me. At that time in his life, he required constant care, and to give my mother a break, he was coming to spend some time in our home with my family. After arriving at his home and getting him settled in my car, we began our two-hour drive to my house. When I turned on the car, the conversational Spanish CDs I was listening to began to play, and he heard the CD of my Spanish lessons. My father had cancer in his throat, and for many years he did have any vocal cords, he spoke with a small voice machine that he held to his throat which produced a tremendously difficult to understand computerized tone. Once he heard the CDs, he got excited and wanted me to get him a copy of French lessons. He told me how he always wanted to learn French and he went on to admit that it may be very difficult at his age and with his current speech challenges. Nevertheless, he has established a culture of cultivating himself for eighty-five years and apparently had no intention of rejecting an opportunity to learn and grow when presented with the chance to do so. It goes without saying that I was motivated by his dedication to develop and pursue growth despite his condition and age. By the way, I couldn't wait to order those CDs for him!

My father's actions in the car that day had such an effect on me that I now realize that as mentors, teachers, and parents, we need to make our process of cultivation public. This is the most effective way to model and motivate duplication of the good habit of being accountable to self-development in the seeds we are growing.

As parents, teachers, and mentors, it is also necessary to create a habit and culture of cultivation within ourselves in order to keep up with the never-ending societal shifts that have caused fashion, literacy, and behavioral differences in the lives of each generation. For instance, when I was a boy, it was understood that we respected our elders even when they were dead wrong, so we followed directions without question or comment. Not so with today's seed. As a whole, they believe respect is earned and not given; and this rule applies to everyone despite age, gender, or position. Today's seeds have limited respect for authority and position but great respect for the concept of respect. Therefore, any authority figure will get much more done through today's youth by engaging them collaboratively in their own development to stimulate bidirectional communication. The trick is to give something of yourself first before expecting respect in return. This brings us full circle to the application of the definition of cultivation.

## Start with What You Expect the Harvest to Look Like

In 1990, Steven Covey wrote the outstanding book *The Seven Habits of Highly Effective People*. Two habits continuously leap out at me, confirming that even the sower needs cultivating:

- (Habit 5) Seek to understand before being understood (Covey 1990)
- (Habit 2) Start with the end in mind (Covey 1990)

Both of these imply the assumption of preparation on the behalf of the mentor, parent, or educator as sowers for effective change to take place.

As parents and mentors, we must deliberately find a way into that alternate reality or secret society our seeds create with their friends and peers. We must learn the foreign language that exists in that communication system. I say push into that realm, not to be an intruder to control it but to seek to understand it by respecting their culture. This will take some biting of the tongue and plenty of counting to ten before speaking, but it will result in opening the ears of your children to your wisdom as they will view you as a part of their reality and not an outsider. Once you do the cultivating work and seek to understand before being understood and they accept you in their world, you can strategically drop pearls of wisdom that will serve as lights that illuminate their paths as they negotiate life.

As parents and mentors, start with the end in mind. You can submit yourselves to researching high-demand careers to help educate your children's dreams toward employable outcomes. Parents can learn about colleges and universities by visiting websites and regularly communicating information about them to their seed to demystify the postsecondary school arena. Parents and mentors can attend seminars or call universities to learn about application processes, entrance exam requirements, and financial aid availability and access. Your open act of self-cultivation will create an attitude in the seed you serve that the next level of education and career development is necessary and not out of reach, thus catapulting more of our urban youth into these experiences. Another example of cultivating parents and mentors as a sower is to study the thinking of other parents who have successfully facilitated their own seed to pursue a path that enables their purpose to flourish. Mimic their actions and implement their big ideas and concepts within the soil you are providing for the seed you are growing. If it is working for them, it will probably work for you.

As educators, we must be open to research as our world is driven by data, assessment, and results. High Poverty, High Performing school (HP2) research is available to give proven strategies and guidance specifically designed to serve our urban and poor rural arenas. Education is one of the fast evolving fields on the planet. If one wants to be effective in education, cultivation must be a way of life.

Although I spoke about professional development and some of the missed marks concerning its implementation a little earlier in this chapter, I want to further that discussion. Classroom walkthroughs are a popular method leaders are utilizing to gather real-time data that assesses instructional practices and thus transform into meaningful PD for the school as a whole. As awesome as this process is, it is rendered useless if educators do not recognize the need to be continually cultivated so they can grow seeds. Just as I had to recultivate my little garden in my backyard each year by raking, hoeing, removing the rocks, and creating rows before dropping the seeds, educators must stay pliable and teachable by actively submitting to ongoing, cultivating self-development opportunities.

## Vantage Point

In the movie *Vantage Point*, each of the main characters had a different reality in their minds about the same series of events that occurred on the day of the main event of the movie. The reality each character experienced was developed solely on the vantage point from which that character was positioned during the event. As the movie developed, the secret service officer played by Kevin Costner, whose mission was to protect the president of the United States, connected pieces of the puzzle together to discover what was actually happening. This occurred as he was exposed to bits and pieces of communication that connected ideas and caused him to change his position or vantage point so he could be more effective in his assignment as a secret service officer and thus achieve his purpose of protecting the president, by all means necessary.

Educators must do what Kevin Costner did in the movie—be alert to the subtle communication being shared with them from the seeds they are growing and the environment in which those seeds are growing. This is no easy task as these communiqués are constant and vary so greatly that it takes time to train one's senses to be aware and able to absorb what is being revealed. This reinforces the fact that urban educators in particular must be willing to remove any resistance to be cultivated to a new way of delivering services to the seeds they are growing. In fact, educators should seek out opportunities to develop, grow, refine, and pursue a greater understanding of big ideas and concepts academically, socially, and behaviorally as they apply to the art of teaching to achieve their ultimate purpose of growing seeds. The mission of educators across the country has not changed in general concept for the last fifty years, but to be effective, the approach to that mission must change on a consistent basis.

In order for sowers to accept the importance for the need to be cultivated, we must be honest, open, and willing:

- Honest to ourselves that there is room for improvement in our instructional, mentoring or parenting skill set, no matter how well our seed are growing.
- Open to the exposure to new and different ideas or concepts that apply to our purpose, despite how uncomfortable that input may be or how blind we are to its validity.
- Willing to do the work to develop an understanding of what is required of us, even if it means changing our vantage point to abandon what we previously accepted as law.

The growth of our seeds is dependent upon the growth of the sower. For the sake of the seeds, even the sower needs cultivating!

## Chapter Recap

Chapter 7    Even the Sower Needs Cultivating
- Origin of the word *cultivate*
- The principle of reciprocity
  - Principles are undoable
  - Are you applying the correct principles to grow our seed?
- Sometimes you have to become the ground so the seed can begin multiplying
  - At eighty-five years old, my father was seeking opportunities to continue personal development and growth

- Societal shifts occur with the generational changing of the guard and impact things like fashion, literary, and behavioral choices
  - Stephen Covey's seven habits of highly effective people
    - Habits two and habits five assume a preparation to change
- Ways for parents and mentors to cultivate themselves
- Ways for educators cultivate themselves
- The conclusion of the whole matter is to be honest, open, and willing

## Chapter Questions

1. What are your thoughts on professional development as a requirement to be a master teacher? What should it entail, how should it be conducted, how long should it be, how can its mastery be measured?
2. Describe an example of an opportunity to *push into* the alternate reality or secret society our seeds create. What are the advantages and disadvantages?
3. Create a list of techniques that you will commit to as a parent, educator, or mentor to cultivate yourself.
4. Discuss the Honest, Open, and Willing approach. Synthesize a scenario that may call for you to apply this principle to yourself so you are able to grow your seeds.

# CHAPTER 8

# THE GREATEST GROWTH HAPPENS TOGETHER

## Two Schools of Thought

The sum total of my observations throughout my career has led me to believe that there are two schools of thought concerning the collaborative and cooperative growth of seeds and sowers. Prior to 2010, I witnessed more of a top-down type of leadership in industry and the schools in which I was employed. Leaders seemed to work more in the authoritative frame than any other. It was common for leaders to create the vision, derive the plan, and tell each person on the team what to do to make that plan happen. As employees, we offered no resistance because it was easier for us. We usually explained away our leaders' dictatorship-type approach by saying that's why they make the "big bucks." However, in the past seven or eight years, the schools I have been affiliated with have been transforming their cultures by activating strategies such as:

- hiring more collaborative leaders
- promoting professional learning communities
- emphasizing shared visions and departmental missions that stem from the main mission
- deliberately building leadership capacity by sharing responsibility and decision making.

This drastic and bold implementation and paradigm shift manifests as a noticeable increase in the math and reading scores that students are achieving on state assessments. These increases can be credited to the hard work students are investing in their education. However, we must also give large amount of credit to educators who have been working hard on their own professional development to grow and hone their skills and instructional delivery strategies.

Although I do not have any empirical research to reinforce the paragraph above, I chose to include it anyway to make a point that as mentors, parents, and educators, our experiences influence the outcome the seeds we are growing will produce. We need to take time (formally or informally) to reflect upon our experiences, learn from them, admit what we need to change, where we need to grow, make those adjustments, and share that we have made them to the seeds we are growing. This cycle of continuous improvement aligns with the Shewart Cycle—"Plan, Do, Study, Act" (Blankstein 2004)—and two immediate results occur when we activate it. We free ourselves to grow and we model to the seeds how to grow.

## What Does Research Say?

As you can tell from the paragraph above, I am biased toward the concept of growing together. Therefore, it seemed wise to provide some research for you to examine to derive your own conclusion about exposing your learning experience to the seeds you are growing. Many adults believe exposing their deficiencies and areas in which they need to grow will be perceived as a weakness to the young seeds they are mentoring. Actually, just the opposite occurs. When you expose your weaknesses and you are transparent about the work you are doing to strengthen that weakness, the seeds who are watching you see the weakness, but it is overshadowed by the strength you are exhibiting to conquer it. Furthermore, they are motivated by your willingness to show them how to win if they are ever confronted by the same or similar challenges. It has been my experience that the greatest growth happens together!

For all of the academic folks reading this book, I thought it would make sense to share with you a splattering of research-based evidence showing the causality between the professional development in which educators participate and student achievement.

## Texas A&M University

The Department of Teaching, Learning, and Culture at Texas A&M University conducted a three-year study titled "The Impact of Sustained Professional Development in STEM on Outcome Measures in a Diverse Urban District." In this study, quantitative and qualitative data was collected to show connections between the professional development of teachers and student achievement.

Sustained professional development can support STEM (Science, Technology, Engineering, and Mathematics) reform. The authors describe a 3-year study of sustained professional development for 3 diverse urban schools across the salient factors of fidelity of implementation of project-based learning, development of professional learning communities, and student achievement. Qualitative and quantitative data were collected. The students who experienced the greatest fidelity of implementation exhibited the greatest gains on standardized test scores, while those with the lowest fidelity of implementation exhibited negative. Qualitative data indicated teachers perceived there were multiple benefits from the implementation of project-based learning. (Capraro, et al. 2016)

## Educational Testing Service

An *Education Week* article published in 2004 highlights the effects the professional development activities teachers participated in was a factor in increasing student achievement:

In a 2000 study of effective teacher practices, a researcher for the Educational Testing Service linked higher student test scores in math with teachers' professional-development training in higher-order thinking skills—for example, devising strategies to solve different types of problems—and in working with special populations of students. The study found a similar jump in science-test scores in connection with teachers who had professional-development training in hands-on laboratory skills. The study's data suggest that other, more all-purpose types of training content like classroom management, interdisciplinary instruction, and collaborative learning had a minimal effect on student scores. (Wenglinsky 2000)

## The National Writing Project

The National Writing Project (NWP) is committed to improving writing and learning in our nation's schools. They have facilitated the implementation of several professional development series and strategic packages. They have monitored teacher and student progress quantitatively and qualitatively to determine if any statistically significant growth occurs with the NWP students and teachers as opposed to the control group of non-NWP students and teachers. The NWP has conducted four statewide studies and at least seven smaller studies in a mixture of urban, suburban, and rural school districts (NWP 2010).

> All of the studies employed pre and post measures of student writing, comparing the performance of students whose teachers had participated in NWP programming to that of students whose teachers had not. Every study involved the direct assessment of student writing, independently scored at a national scoring conference where the Analytic Writing Continuum (NWP 2006, 2008) was applied with considerable reliability and technical rigor" (NWP 2010).

In each study, students have yielded statistically significant positive gains in their writing pre- and postassessments while the control group has yielded minimal gains and in some cases, losses on the same assessments. Teachers were also evaluated qualitatively by comparing their survey results to the performance of their students. The NWP is another example of the need for sowers to grow, so the seeds they tend to can grow as well. Please feel free to view the report yourself at http://www.nwp.org/cs/public/print/resource/3208 to see proof that the greatest growth happens together.

## Council of Chief State School Officers

In another study (Blank and de Las Alas 2012), the Council of Chief State School Officers (CCSSO) was awarded a grant from the National Science Foundation to conduct a meta-analysis study ( a meta-analysis is a large study done on a collection of smaller studies) to provide scientifically based evidence regarding the effects of teacher professional development on improving student learning. The analysis included sixteen studies that focused on the effects of professional development for science and mathematics teachers on the K-12 level. The meta-analysis results show that teacher professional development in mathematics has a significant positive effect on student achievement. The experimental group had a mean effect on post assessments of 0.21. This nearly doubled the mean effect of 0.13 the control group scored on postassessments. The analysis result also confirms the positive relationship to student outcomes of key characteristics of design of professional development programs (Blank and de Las Alas 2009).

## Okay, Okay, Enough of the Research Stuff

This chapter was meant to reinforce chapter 7. The strategy was to provide some scientifically based evidence, hoping to reinforce the idea that mentors, parents, and educators should have about being transparent in their own learning process. It is perfectly okay to be cultivated and to let the seeds we are growing know that we are being cultivated, just as they are. We are in this thing together. If done correctly and made a part of the culture of our cultivation process, we will enhance the growth of our seeds by creating a relationship of trust, nurture, and high expectation because what we are asking them to do, we are doing for ourselves in plain sight. We must not be afraid to discuss with our seed the thought process that aids our own learning curve and we should often think aloud so they can hear how we make connections and synthesize new ideas. Some call this process brain-based learning, some call it scaffolding, some call it the zone of proximal development; whatever title you give this process, it is cultivation—moving from one state of being to another.

So the moral of the story is, no matter whether you are a parent, mentor, or educator, you should with a sense of urgency and transparency to seek opportunities to cultivate yourself by reading books and articles; discussing hot topics; listening to lectures; creating support groups and professional learning communities; attending formal sessions; or creating your own informal sessions in your homes, offices, or classrooms to become deliberate about being consciously competent in perfecting the methodologies you use to grow your seeds. Submit to and share your own *growth* journey with your seeds. Modeling how you grow will help stimulate your seeds to do what is necessary to maximize their own *growth* processes. The greatest *growth* happens together!

## Chapter Recap

Chapter 8    The Greatest Growth Happens Together
- There were two schools of thought concerning collaborative growth
  - Top-down method
  - Collaborative method
- Strengths or weaknesses of collaborative growth
- Less recent philosophy supports top-down leadership with the leader is infallible
- Recent research shows that collaborative leadership style is more conducive to growth

## Chapter Questions

1. Interpret the Shewart cycle, giving examples of how it appears in your organization.
2. Tell what you liked about two of the research instances featured in this chapter. Explain why they appeal to you.
3. Share your thoughts about the idea that the seeds' growth is directly proportionate to your own growth.

# CHAPTER 9

# Make the Seed Aware of Their Seeds

## Everything Has Its Own DNA

Accroding to researchers, every corn seed when planted and properly brought to maturity can produce a stalk that yields four to six ears of corn. When mature, approximately six hundred kernels are produced on each of those ears (Elmore and Abendroth 2006). Each of those kernels is a seed with the ability to produce another stalk with the same capabilities of the stalk that produced it. The harvest cycle is self-perpetuated such that the kernels of corn that fall to the ground can germinate and continue the cycle by producing another plant on their own. This is called procreation. By design, every creature in nature has the potential and the inherent purpose to procreate. This cycle of seeding, time, and harvest will continue until the creator stop it.

Every organic or living creature possesses DNA that defines its characteristics, such that each creature reproduces after its own kind. Not to get too scientific, but in short, the DNA of a thing determines the details of its being and more importantly, what it will possess to accomplish its purpose. The seeds we are growing have their own seeds within, and they can and want to reproduce. For instance, our urban centers are full of people of color; and to highlight some of the achievements of the African Americans in particular, in urban areas, we can look to Halle Salosie, Granville Woods, Lewis Latimere, Charles Drew, Madame C.J. Walker, Fredrick Douglas, and Elijah McCoy, just to name a few. Each of these people had the seeds within themselves to invent something that has changed how our modern society exists across the globe. Although most of their accomplishments were introduced many years ago, their seeds have procreated by morphing through the gifting of people who have improved on their original ideas. Likewise, the seeds we are parenting, educating, and mentoring are destined to be greater than us if we grow them correctly.

## Urban Realities

Unfortunately, the seedlings we are growing in our urban homes, communities, and schools are often unaware of the giftedness, talents, visions, and purposes that they possess within. This very common phenomenon can be contributed to three unfortunate realties of the urban community:

1. Hopes for our seeds are shadowed by acres of fields of unprofitable crops that make dark possibilities the norm. Drugs, alcohol, poverty, substandard living conditions, miseducation, abuse, poor health conditions, crime, aborted dreams and disappointments are reproduced in large quantities and are therefore accentuated and become norms and thus expectations in the minds of our seeds.

2. Our seeds are victims of a belief system of limitations and ceilings set by a majority culture that does not live by the same basic rules of our urbanized seeds. I use the term "belief system" because it does not have to be a written decree or conscious effort to limit others. It can be long-lived and accepted patterns of thinking that cause us to act in ways that support limiting others without even knowing we are actually doing so.

3. Exposure to alternative ways of thinking and living and the encouragement to be courageous enough to step out of the box to invest in their own possibilities is lacking in the lives of our urbanized seeds. To counteract this lack of exposure and encouragement, our seeds must be flooded with a constant message that what they physically see is not all they can be. They must be taught to move toward possibilities that are manifested by their own abilities and purposes.

## Monkeys in a Room

The following was introduced to me by my Educational Psychology professor while I was earning my master's degree in education leadership at York College. Although I cannot find any evidence that this is an actual study, I totally agree with what it implies and encourage you to meditate on its message as well. The story, which again I cannot confirm that it actually occurred, says that there was a study done many years ago that included four monkeys in a glass room with only a pole in the center of the room and a bunch of bananas at the top of the pole. When one of the monkeys would try to climb the pole and get a banana, a powerful jet of cold water would spray the monkey that was trying to climb the pole and every other monkey in the room as well. The jet was so powerful that it would knock the climbing monkey off of the pole back onto the floor, and in addition to the cold water, an unpleasant shock was also administered to the monkeys. The four monkeys tried over and over to get the bananas to no avail, and after several weeks of the cold jets of water and unpleasant shocks, they lost their will to even try to get the bananas any longer. Instead, the four monkeys simply waited to be fed by their human captives, if and when the humans decided to do so.

The study continued by removing one of the four original monkeys and replacing it with another monkey that had never been in the room before. The new monkey instinctively went to climb the pole to get the bananas and the other three monkeys violently attacked it to prevent it from climbing the pole. As one would expect, the new monkey was determined the get those bananas and tried over and over to climb the pole. Each time, the three remaining monkeys violently attacked it until the new monkey lost its will to climb the pole and simply waited to be fed by its human captors, if and when the humans decided to do so.

The study continued by repeating the process of removing each of the original monkeys one by one and replacing them with a monkey that had never been in the room before. Each new monkey tried to climb the pole and was violently attacked by the other three monkeys. After several months, the room was filled with all new monkeys and none of them would climb the pole. As an added measure, one of the four second-generation monkeys who had never been sprayed by the cold water or shocked when the pole was approached was replaced with a third-generation monkey, and lo and behold, the three second generation monkeys violently attacked the third generation monkey when it tried to climb the pole.

Let's take a minute to review a few things and parallel the experiences of the monkeys to how the mindsets of our seeds could be shaped by their urban environments.

- Monkeys like bananas but don't like powerful jets of cold water that knock them off of poles or unpleasant electrical shocks. (*Realities of the environment overshadow inherent desires.*)
- The attacking monkeys were only trying to protect themselves and the new monkey from the powerful jets of cold water and unpleasant electrical shocks. (*Conditioned to accept the ceiling set for them by the response of their physical surroundings when they pursued change.*)
- Remember, they knew that their human captors would feed them, or at least believed they would. (*Welfare or slave mentality—conditioned to wait for someone to offer a solution to their issue rather than finding a solution themselves.*)
- After a while, the monkeys didn't even know why climbing the pole was a no-no. (*Norms of the community were accepted despite the fact that they didn't make sense.*)
- The second- and third-generation monkeys never experienced the powerful cold jets of water or unpleasant electrical shocks (*external factors*). They only felt the attack of the other monkeys (*community-based factors*). (*We are both our own problem and own our solution.*)

The study was furthered when a switch was uncovered in the same room, which turned the water on and off. The monkeys were now armed with the knowledge that they could control the external factors, but this was not enough to make any of the monkeys climb the pole because although they knew they had the ability to climb it, they did not believe they had the right to climb it to retrieve the bananas. The ability to turn the water off and on was not specific enough to counteract the culture that existed in the room. One of the human captors had to place one of the monkeys on the pole after the water was turned off by one of the other monkeys. The human captor experienced a great amount of resistance from the monkey, but once one monkey was convinced to climb the pole after the switch was turned off, the other three monkeys quickly followed. After all, every monkey has the inherent ability to climb, and likes bananas. They simply needed to know the possibility was *meant for them* to achieve and attain.

## Our Seeds Need to Know

The seeds we are growing need to know within themselves that they have the ability to change their circumstances. They need to know that they have the power to change their homes, their communities, and their cities. Despite our success or failures financially, educationally, in our careers, relationships, or social status, this is one of the most important things we as mentors, parents, and educators are able implant in our seeds. What you have done with your life has nothing to do with your ability to help your seeds. We don't have to be an expert at climbing poles to place our seed on the pole so they can climb it. Just like the human who had to place the single monkey on the pole to show all the monkeys that they could climb and get the bananas at the top, all we have to do is intervene and fight the existing culture, with great respect, to show our seeds that they can climb the poles in front of them and attain their goals. When we are courageous enough to do so, our seed will realize their inherent abilities and desires and grow toward their aspirations and purpose simply because they now know they can.

Our seeds need to know:

- They have inherent abilities specific to themselves that make them valuable and unique

- The inherent abilities each seeds possess are intended for them to achieve a purpose that is meant to add not only to them but to their community as well
- The purpose with which each seed is charged is destined to produce their fruit in the form of contributions to society.
- The fruit each seed manifests contains more seeds with the purpose of affecting the lives of others and allowing them to achieve their purpose, thus creating a continuous cycle that procreates positivity.

As mentors, parents. and educators, we have to be deliberate in making our seeds aware of their seeds. Choose strategies and method-ologies that allow for the activation of self-actualization within the seed you are growing. Find ways to create project-based learning scenarios that stimulate your seed to explore their creativity, leadership skills, strengths, weaknesses, adaptability, application of principled concepts, innovation, and ability to apply their ideas to tasks that will not only help solidify mastery of intended content but add to the quality of life of those around them. This will stimulate an intrinsic desire to grow and step outside of the box of traditional and sometimes over-whelming shadows to achieve their purpose because of the realization that it—their purpose—has become important, not only to their own advancement but that of others as well. This new responsibility-driven belief system will counteract the inhibiting forces in the community and the relationships that exist therein. This paradigm shift in belief systems will catapult our once limited seeds into a process of growing to learn and away from the rote traditions of learning to grow.

## Exposure Is the First Step to Change!

If we want our urban seeds to change the path that has been carved for them by the dark shadows that exist in the culture of their community, we have to induce systemic change that focuses on exposure and stimulation of new paradigms in the belief systems of the unproductive crops our urban areas have harvested in the past. Very simply, if you are an educator, the change I am referring to has to begin with the school leaders, preferably central administration. If the leaders are not cultivating the ground and maximizing growth, there is no way that the rest of the organization can possibly do so. In essence, the dichotomy of the organization (leadership and workforce) will begin to eat the same hoagie from two different ends and eventually find themselves face to face chomping at each other. Sound familiar?

If you are a parent, you and your spouse must totally agree on your approach to change the thinking of your seed and align to change the rules of the household down to the type of conversations you allow in your home. You must recreate the culture of your home so possibilities and the work it takes to accomplish those possibilities are prevalent in the cultural atmosphere within it. If you are a community mentor, you have to rally support from other community members to create regular meetings in a public places that are common knowledge for all generations in your neighborhood. Your objective is to create a force that is regaining your seeds by uniting and helping each other to take a similar stand in their own households. Your community-wide common mission is to motivate seeds to reach their full potential and help others to do the same.

## We Can't Make Them Aware of What We Don't Know

We must make the seed aware of their seeds. But this cannot take place until *we* are aware of their seeds. As mentioned in a previous chapter, the most powerful mind-set one can employ that will allow anyone to see the capabilities of any seed is Steven Covey's habit number five, "*seeking to understand before being understood*" (Covey 1990). This habit makes us a sponge to every detail of our surroundings, rather than a paint brush trying to create the surrounding. As teachers, parents, and mentors, to better understand our seeds' potential, we should take an approach that employs strategies such as:

- Socratic discussion
- think pair share
- if this changes, what then . . .

- what would you do if . . .
- partner and team work
- the Shewart Cycle: Plan, Do, Study Act (Blankstein 2004)
- a culminating project
- an opportunity to present or share their ideas

Before you say, "I've tried that," or "that's what I do and it doesn't work," take a moment to reflect on your own effectiveness. Get ready for this statement because it may sting a little: *Maybe you're just not as good at growing seeds as you think you are.* Hence, the chapter explaining that even the sower needs cultivating is important to your development. Remember someone was relentless in doing the same things for you. Now it's your turn to give back, or maybe you need to rethink your position as a mentor of any type!

At the drop of a dime, we should be able to sit down and discuss the strengths, weaknesses, and strategies that create a positive return for each of our seeds. This is our reasonable service. However, if we want to affect real change, we have to be able to activate those discussions into practice systemically, strategically, and with all diligence and perseverance. That's correct; *we have to fight to make our seed aware of the seeds within them.* Quite frankly, if you're not willing to go the distance with this fight, you should get out of the race as you will be killing seeds before they get the chance to germinate and reach the surface! I make that statement with great conviction as I unequivocally believe this is a hill upon which I proclaim all parents, mentors, and educators should die.

Make no mistake, as mentors, parents, and educators the survival and growth of our seeds is dependent upon our ability to synergize encouragement, exposure, and preparation. Encouragement is a source of courage that comes from within—en-courage-ment. We have the ability to get inside of our seeds' self-image and bellow air to the flames of their courageousness, causing those flames to swell and heat up the intensity to which our seeds approach their possibilities from the inside out.

Our seeds will not grow not because they alone think they can grow; they will not grow because we alone think they can grow. They will grow because they think that we think they can grow. Take time to tell your seeds what you think and what you see when you look at them, what gifts they possess, and how you expect great things from them. This kind of constant watering and fertilizing of the ground helps untangle our urban seeds from the weeds in their communities that are trying to choke and hinder their growth, and frees them to grow uninhibited. Couple that with exposure to the things that are usually thought to be too advanced or socially out of reach for our urban seeds. Things that stimulate curiosity and demystify the supposedly magical academic content, career path planning, and family relations that the high-performing and more affluent suburban seeds are operating in as a norm. This will produce a generation of seeds that not only believe they can grow, but they will have been exposed to possibilities and put in touch with the inward courage needed to grow toward their purpose.

## This Is a Process

Keep in mind this is not an instantaneous event; it is a process that requires patience, perseverance, diligence, and stubbornness from parents, educators, and mentors who are sowing into our urban youth. Just as the farmer did in earlier chapters, we must maximize every opportunity to produce a healthy harvest with the self-imposed expectation that we will do just that. Finally, after encouraging and exposing, we must prepare our seeds to conquer those things to which we have exposed them. This means that parents, educators, and mentors must increase the expectations on their seed by monitoring how they talk, who they associate with, the activities in which they participate, how they complete their schoolwork, what their benchmark assessments look like, how they are ranking academically, what colleges they are aspiring to attend, and the list grows as your level of preparation matches your expectations for your seed.

As educators, we are charged with watering, fertilizing, and pulling weeds for our seeds on a daily basis. We must increase our expectations by ramping up the curriculum we deliver to our seeds. Strive to accelerate learning by integrating intervention systems in our schools and classes that help students with specific weaknesses, thereby turning those weaknesses into strengths. In essence, teach *up* and not down.

One of the most revelation-filled moments I had as an educator was when the director of special education (Dr. B.) was explaining how to properly deliver instruction for special education students with accommodations. Prior to her presentation to us, the principals in the school district, my approach was totally incorrect. Until then, I had been very successful in the classroom and as a school leader. However, I was condoning and encouraging teaching down to students as I interpreted accommodations as eliminating the content that *we* thought the Individualized Education Program (IEP) student could not master. I did not understand that accommodations were tools to help the student master the same content as other non-IEP students.

The revelation was that *the expectations for both groups were the same!* When I look back, I feel horrible for the students whom, prior to my encounter with Dr. B., I cheated out of the full potential of the educational experience they deserved. But I feel even worse when I think of the multitude of educators still erroneously operating in the same principle I once did. Unfortunately, many of these educators are still operating in our urban schools, canceling out the great work that their master teacher colleagues are accomplishing in their classrooms.

I charge you to prepare our urban seeds to grow on fields outside of the urban arena. As you do so, keep in mind that you must endure the meticulous process it takes for each seed to develop. Endure the time they need to develop the ability and belief that they have permission to see beyond the urban fields to which they have been confined. These things must occur before they will buy into the synergy you are working to attain. But once they do, and you do, man oh man, the outcomes of the seeds you are growing will have no ceilings. Remember the ultimate goal is to make the seed aware of the seeds they possess.

## Chapter Recap

Chapter 9   Make the Seed Aware of Their Seeds

- A single corn seed can produce a healthy cornstalk that yields anywhere from six to eight ears of healthy corn at a time
- Each ear of corn has approximately six hundred kernels, which are all potential seeds
- As the cycle continues, seeds produce stalks, which produce ears, which produce seeds, which produce more stalks, and the cycle continues until the creator says stop
- By design, everything has the potential to reproduce and the inherent desire to do so
- Things can only reproduce after their own kind
- The seed we have growing have their own seeds within, and they can and want to grow and reproduce
- Urban youth are generally unaware of the seeds they possess
- Urban youth generally do not believe they have permission to pursue and accomplish their dreams, goals, and aspirations
- Making the seed aware of their seeds will stimulate growth, counteracting the inhibiting forces of their urban environment

## Chapter Questions

1. In your own words, write the three reasons why urban youth are usually unaware of the seeds within themselves and the power they harness.
2. Share one message you received from the monkey story and how you can use it to create positive cycles in the seeds you are growing.
3. How do you plan on helping our seeds know the four *need-to-know* bullet points outlined in this chapter?

4. What are some of the details of the belief system in place in your organization? Are they supportive or hindering to the development of the seeds for which you are responsible?
5. Describe how you can create a synergy between encouragement, exposure, and preparation.

# CHAPTER 10

## ROTATE THE CROPS

## My Elementary School Teacher

I remember when I was a young boy in school, a teacher taught us that every few years, most farmers rotate their crops. I had a visual of the farmers picking up every plant and transferring them into another field. I recall thinking, *What is the point of doing all of that work?* When I got enough courage to ask that question to the teacher, she responded by providing the correct picture of rotating the crops, and then she asked me a question that to this day shapes my thinking in powerful ways. She asked, "If what you pictured was correct, and that crop belonged to you, and all of that work was necessary for you to take care of the crop, would that work be worth it?" Little did I know, but she was planting a seed in my little mind that was designed to instill in me what many teachers, coaches, pastors, and family members have repeatedly confirmed throughout my lifetime: *Work in, equals work out!* Even if the farmer really did have to dig up each plant and move it to another field for it to thrive and produce a plenteous harvest, I believe he would do it with no hesitation. A fair question to ponder at this point is, are we willing to do whatever it takes to help the crops we are producing with our lives to survive and thrive?

## What is Crop Rotation?

Crop rotation is the successive cultivation of different crops in a specified order on the same fields. Crop rotation also means that succeeding crops are of a different variety than the previous crop on any particular field. For example, on a particular field, a farmer would plant what are known as row crops after small grains, grain crops after legumes, barley after wheat, and so on. The planned rotation schedule may be for two or three years before the same type of crop is planted on the same field again. Crop rotations are done to improve or maintain soil fertility, reduce erosion, control pests, reduce risk of weather damage, reduce reliance on pesticides, and most importantly, increase harvests and net profits. The downside of crop rotations is that it requires additional planning and management skills, increasing the work the farmer has to do to realize a plenteous and maximized harvest on the fields which he has committed to work.

Now that you are totally bored and trying figure out why I am rambling on about crop rotation, let me tell you my logic. As human beings, we tend to shy away from work, and as the seeds we are growing get mature, more work is required. However, the work shifts from the traditional weeding, watering, and fertilizing to which we have become accustomed, to include more planning and strategic positioning to increase capacity. This is where we tend to fall off as parents, mentors, and educators. I submit to you that your seeds are relying on you to monitor and counsel their growth as they move into their fruit-bearing stages. As a school leader, I routinely surveyed parents and captured participation and attendance data to provide insight into the effectiveness of the home-school-community events we hosted. I discovered a pattern that revealed the intensity of parent participation decrease for students in the sixth grade from 80 percent participation at the beginning of the year to approximately 15 percent by the end of the year. At the same time, sixth-grade students were experiencing an increase in disciplinary referrals and decreasing grades and attendance rates. This alarming data is just one example of the confirmation that our seeds need us far into their maturity just as much as they do when they are yet seedlings.

## From Slaves to the Promised Land

How can we as mentors, educators, and parents decrease the amount of work and increase the assurance that our seeds will continue to grow into their maturity? Simple, learn to rotate the crops. I am a storyteller; and to get my point across, I want to use an example of a great nation of people, their journey from slavery, and their migration to a land that was promised to their ancestors many generations ago.

This great nation of people was conquered and enslaved by a greater empire. The ruler of the greater empire was a hard taskmaster and used these people to build their cities, monuments, aqueducts, palaces, and agriculture systems. One day after much persuasion, the ruler decided to let these people go free. The people left the empire and began traveling to a land that was promised to them. In this land, they intended on settling and building their own culture so they could thrive and provide a home that future generations would be proud of.

There was a great wilderness between the empire and the land to which they were traveling. There were nearly four hundred thousand people from the enslaved nation traveling this difficult journey, and as they traveled to their land, many terrible things happened to them. The ruler of the empire changed his mind and decided to chase them and bring them back. The people ran out of food and water, the children began to grow and their clothes became worn, and they got lost and wandered in the wilderness for years. Despite the fact that a miraculous event occurred to counteract each of the terrible things which they encountered, the people began murmuring and complaining that they should go back to the empire and be slaves because it was easier there.

The leadership was focused on one thing, reaching the Promised Land. However, after forty long years, every adult slave that left the empire that had enslaved them had died in the journey through the wilderness. This means that every person that entered into the Promised Land was just a child when they left that empire and most of their developmental years were spent in the journey through the wilderness. The adults that refused to, or didn't know how to rotate their own crops so they could survive in a different field, literally complained so much that they were unable to learn to adjust. In essence, they complained themselves to death.

Just before entering their Promised Land, the leadership of the former slaves changed, and a new, younger leader who matured during the journey through the wilderness was appointed. He had been watching the previous leader for a while and identified some things that were lacking. So when he was appointed the next leader, he already had an idea of what to do to help the people progress. The biggest difference in his leadership style was that he understood the principle of *rotating the crops*. First, he made sure the history of his people's journey was told repeatedly in the camps so everyone knew and understood what they had endured and walked away from. He wanted everyone to remember what they came out of and the miraculous things that took place along the way to get to the land they now occupy. He understood that this would bring value to their past, meaning to their present, and confidence in the ability to do the work that needed to be done to establish a bright future.

Next, he positioned the people to take what was promised to them. Each battle for their land was organized and strategically planned as the people were given tasks to complete in order for the whole nation to prosper. Finally, he made sure that the younger generation was clear and well-versed on the history of the people and were given opportunities to be trained and contribute to the nation in meaningful ways. This ensured that the work that began could continue after this generation passed away and the younger generation would know what to do and how to do it. Here are the four things the succeeding leader did.

1. He made sure his seeds were going to grow, as he cultivated the ground by making sure the history of the people was known and respected.
2. He assigned a task to each person. This established meaning and value, individually and collectively, and thus stimulated growth and ownership in the nation.
3. He prepared the nation to perpetuate maximized growth by rotating the crops. He made sure that each member of the younger generation had an opportunity to experience leadership and service. Their success with this test made it so they were trusted as it applied to the existence and future leadership of the nation.
4. He created a bank of leaders so as gaps in leadership positions occurred, another person from the younger generation would be immediately accessible and trained to assume that role.

As educators, parents, and mentors, we must learn from this story and make our seeds aware of the struggles of their forefathers and the victories of the progress of their people and communities. These realities should not be shunned and placed away only to be featured on special days (Black History Month, Cinco de Mayo, Hispanic Heritage Month, and so on). They have to be kept in the forefront and used as constant reminders of where our seeds have come from to motivate them to focus on where they are going. It behooves educators to connect to the communities they serve and shed any uncomfortable feelings that arise when discussing cultural and historical issues among the racial and ethnical variety of our urban seeds. This will lead the way to culturally relevant curriculum that aligns with tenets of the Every Student Succeeds Act (ESSA), Common Core Standards, and project-based learning tactics (PBL). These strategic cultural shifts prepare the ground by enlightening us and equipping us with the knowledge of the culture we need to properly rotate our crops on the particular field which we are serving and ensure the harvest from our seeds is maximized.

## What Are the Advantages of Rotating the Crops?

Another outcome from rotating the crops in this manner is that our seeds are encouraged to dream and attach their goals to a vision. Keeping them aware of the shifting of their history from one growing field to another stimulates the thought of possibilities. It reinforces the culture of change, and thus, the belief system of the seeds remains open and willing to move toward new things. Exposure to career possibilities is an important component of rotating the crops. Once our seeds know what they can be, they will want to be those things. To maximize exposure to possibilities, it is imperative that the seeds must know and accept that it is their responsibility to grow toward their goals. Thus, rotating the crops establishes accountability of the learning and doing process by introducing seeds to the reality of what it takes to plan, prepare for, and work to accomplish their goals.

More specifically, as parents, educators, and mentors, we are charged to rotate the crops by preparing our seed for leadership instances and experiences. In many cases, we will have to take time to adjust our usual approach to growing our seeds and include additional planning to create leadership opportunities in which our seeds can participate. They should be meaningful and impactful to the social climate in which we are growing our seeds to be an effective tool for learning and training. Not only should these opportunities be impactful, they should be designed to train the next generation for continuance of the forward progress the seeds who came before them have made. In other words, nothing's permanent. Everything is built on the premise of rotating the crops to avoid stagnancy, depletion of necessary creativity, and the overworking or reliance upon any one section of the soil.

In rotating our crops, it give us as educators, parents, and mentors the opportunity to ensure that all areas of our seeds' lives are being enriched. As we rotate opportunities for our seeds, we as well as they will begin to see strengths and weaknesses that exist within them. Rotation illuminates the gifts within our seeds and allows us to encourage them to operate in those gifts. It also affords us the ability to prepare our seeds to flourish on any field by teaching them to rely upon their abilities as further rotation occurs when our seeds leave our care and progress throughout life. Let's be realistic. By rotating the crops, we will cause the root and foundation of our seeds some discomfort. However, this in turn strengthens them and catapults their growth into another realm of prosperity. These tactics nurture the growth of our seeds and turn the past trends of perpetuated poverty into perpetuated prosperity. I have to ask, how hard are you willing to work for that?

Finally, from the beginning of our preparation process as we break up the fallow ground that is mentioned in chapter 1, we have to establish a culture for our seeds that screams out loud their ability to prosper in different fields and contribute in productive ways to those fields. Our seed must accept and expect that where they are now is not their final destination. They are only here with us to get them ready for the next field so they can compete with other seedlings and successfully negotiate the challenges that await them as they grow. This will not be an easy task if we do not submit to Covey's fifth habit and seek to understand before being understood. Once that trust is established, almost anything we want to engraft in our seedlings and anywhere we want to take them will be just fine with them. Rotate the crops and expand the horizons our seeds can imagine. You will not only free them from the slavery of perpetuated poverty and socioeconomic distress, you will also help them grow forward, increasing the probability that they will get to live in their Promised Land. Rotate the crops!

## Chapter Recap

Chapter 10    Rotate the Crops
- Farmers rotate the crops
  - to keep the soil nutrient rich
  - with calculated planning with the deliberate purpose of ensuring growth
- A nation of people's freedom from slavery
- The new leader learned what was missing by watching the old leader.
  - told the history of the people
  - gave everyone a task
  - trained youth for future tasks
  - created a bank of possible leaders
- Make our seeds aware of past and possible futures
  - Parents and mentors should tell their story
  - Schools should teach culturally relevant curriculum
- Encourage the seeds to dream
  - Educate about career choices
  - Make connections to the seeds role in those dreams
- We must rotate our crops
  - Prepare for leadership
  - Make instances for leadership opportunities
  - Training for continuance
  - Ensure that all areas of our seeds lives are being enriched
  - Nurture growth and prosperity as a plan
  - Grow our seeds so they have the ability to prosper in different fields and contribute

## Chapter Questions

1. What are some of the explicit differences in approaches when supporting more mature seeds?

2. One of the morsels in the story of the people who were freed from slavery was that the first leader, although tremendously focused on the agreed-upon destination, did not rotate crops to build capacity. Elaborate on how important is that lesson in what you do with your seeds.

3. Do you feel comfortable talking about ethnicity and race-centered topics with all of the seeds you are growing? Do you think this is important? Why?

4. How are you already rotating the crops?

5. How can you increase your ability to rotate the crops?

6. When rotating your crops, what types of things do you do to prepare your seeds to exist and thrive on different fields outside of the normal community settings?

# BIBLIOGRAPHY

Chapter 1

Rideout, P. M. *Newberry House Dictionary of American English* (4th ed.). (Boston: Thompson, 2004).

Chapter 2

Rideout, P. M. *Newberry House Dictionary of American English* (6th ed.). (Boston: Thompson, 2016)

Chapter 3

"Learning Disabilities: An Overview." LD Online, retrieved on April 7, 2011, http://www.ldonline.org/article/Learning_Disabilities%3A_An_Overview

Lewis, C.W. "African American Male Discipline Patterns and School District Responses Resulting Impact on Academic Achievement: Implications for Urban Educators and Policy Makers." *Journal of African American Males in Education* 1, no. 1(2010).

"A 25 Year History of the IDEA." US Department of Education, retrieved on April 7, 2011, http://www2.ed.gov/policy/speced/leg/idea/history.pdf

Chapter 4

Zhao, C., G. D. Kuh, and R. M. Carini. "A Comparison of International Student and American Student Engagement in

Effective Educational Practices." *The Journal of Higher Education* 76, no. 2(2005): 209–231. doi:10.1353/jhe.2005.0018

## Chapter 5

Achieve (2009). "Race to the Top: Accelerating College and Career Readiness in States—Low-Performing Schools. retrieved from https://www.achieve.org/RTTT-Low-PerformingSchools

Greene, J. and M. A. Winters. "Leaving Boys Behind: Public High School Graduation Rates" [Civic Report #48]. New York: Manhattan Institute for Policy Research. 2006

McDermott, P., and J. J. Rothenburg. "Why Urban Parents Resist Involvement in Their Children's Elementary Education," *The Qualitative Report* 5, no. 3(2000): 1–16. Retrieved from https://nsuworks.nova.edu/tqr/vol5/iss3/4

"Trends in High School Dropout and Completion Rates in the United States." National Center for Education Statistics. (2017), https://nces.ed.gov/programs/ dropout/ind_02.asp

"High School Benchmarks 2016: National College Progression Rates," National Student Clearinghouse Research Center, last modified December 18, 2017, https://nscresearchcenter.org/high-school-benchmarks-2016-national-college-progression-rates

Sanford, S. "Preparing All Young People for College, Work and Citizenship," *The State Education Standard* 7, no. 2(2017): 4–5. Arlington, VA: National Association of State Boards of Education.

University of Chicago. "Lack Of Trust Leads To Dysfunctional School Systems," ScienceDaily. last modified August 27, 2012, www.sciencedaily.com/releases/2008/08/080827164035.htm.

Zenkov, K. "Seeing the Pedagogies, Practices, and Programs Urban Students Want," *Theory Into Practice* 48 (2009): 168–175.

## Chapter 7

Covey, S. *The Seven Habits of Highly Effective People*. (Free Press: Tampa, 1990).

Rideout, P. M. *Newberry House Dictionary of American English* (6th ed.). (Boston: Thompson, 2014).

Chapter 8

Blank, Rolf K, and Nina de Las Alas (2009). *The Effects of Teacher Professional Development on Gains in Student Achievement: How Meta-Analysis Provides Scientific Evidence Useful to Education Leaders.* Council of Chief State School Officers. Retrieved June 23, 2009, from https://files.eric.ed.gov/fulltext/ED544700.pdf.

Capraro, R. M., M. M. Capraro, J. J. Scheurich, M. Jones, J. Morgan, K. S. Huggins, S. Han. "Impact of Sustained Professional Development in STEM on Outcome Measures in a Diverse Urban District." *The Journal of Educational Research* 109, no. 2(2016): 181–196. doi:10.1080/00220671.2014.936997

Darling-Hammond, L. "Teacher Learning That Supports Learning," *Educational Leadership*, 1998.

Darling-Hammond, L. and M. W. McLaughlin. "Policies That Support Professional Development in an Era of Reform," *Phi Delta Kappan*, 1995. Reprint by MiddleWeb.

"Professional Development," *Education Week*, retrieved on June 3, 2011, http://www.edweek.org/ew/issues/professional-development.

Kennedy, M.M., "Measuring Progress Toward Equity in Science and Mathematics Education," *Wisconsin Center for Education Research*, 1998.

"Every Child Reading: A Professional Development Guide," *Learning First Alliance*, 2000.

Little, J.W., "Teachers Professional Development in a Climate of Education Reform," U.S. Department of Education, 1994.

Miles, M. B., "Forward," *Professional Development in Education: New Paradigms and Practices*, edited by Thomas Guskey and Michael Huberman. Teachers College Press, 1995.

"Teacher Preparation and Professional Development: 2000," National Center for Education Statistics, 2001.

"What Matters Most: Teaching for America's Future," National Commission on Teaching & America's Future, 1996.

"Research Brief: Writing Project Professional Development Continues to Yield Gains in Student Writing Achievement," *National Writing Project* 2 (2010).

Porter, A.C., B.F. Birman, and M.S. Garet. "Does Professional Development Change Teaching Practice? Results From a Three-Year Study," 2000. See "Executive Summary."

Smylie, M.A., E. Allensworth, R.C. Greenberg, R. Harris, and S. Luppescu. "Teacher Professional Development in Chicago: Supporting Effective Practice," *Consortium on Chicago School Research*, 2001.

Wenglinsky, H. "How Teaching Matters: Bringing the Classroom Back Into Discussions of Teacher Quality," *Educational Testing Service*, 2000.

"Teachers Who Learn, Kids Who Achieve: A Look at Schools With Model Professional Development," *WestED* 2000.

Chapter 9

Covey, S. *The Seven Habits of Highly Effective People*. (Free Press: Tampa, 1990).

Elmore, R., and L. Abendroth. "To Be Determined: Ear Row Numbers and Kernels Per Row in Corn," *Integrated Crop Management* 496, no. 13(2006): 151–152.

Blankstein, A. *Failure Is Not an Option*. (Thousand Oaks: Corwin, 2004).

Chapter 10

Peel, M. D. "Crop Rotations for Increased Productivity." retrieved from http://www.ag.ndsu.edu/pubs/plantsci/crops/eb48-1.htm.

# ABOUT THE AUTHOR

D r. Newton H. Miller II is a husband and father of seven productive young adults. He has earned a BA in Mathematics, minoring in Physics, a MEd in Education Leadership, an MBA with a focus in Marketing, and a PhD in Education Administration. He has committed over twenty years of his life to the education arena by serving as a middle school and high school mathematics and science teacher and a principal of both middle and high schools in low-performing urban school districts. He has written plans to establish and expand alternative learning settings for disruptive students, helped create and teach remedial math programs on the community college level, consulted in several alternative high schools across the country, and now serves as a professor of education at Ashford University, where he leads a team that builds teacher preparation programs focusing on preparing effective educators to serve all students, but particularly urban and at-risk learners.

Dr. Miller's passion is to help others visualize and activate themselves to call forth their own potential to fulfill their purpose in life. Thus, his mantra and ulterior motive is always to educate, motivate, and help them grow. After facing many challenges, roadblocks, and self-dug pitfalls which he had to conquer and overcome in his own life, Dr. Miller has dedicated his research and professional practices to finding what works in educating nontraditional and at-risk populations.

Dr. Miller has led teams that have revolutionized high-poverty, low-performing schools to reverse their pattern of failure by dismantling and rebuilding school culture, home-school-community relations, and the efficacy of educators and students individually and collectively. Throughout the years, he has been active in local ministries focusing on educating and empowering young people (young men in particular) by encouraging and supporting educational attainment, emphasizing vision, purpose, and self-esteem, and organizing rites of passage programming.

One of Dr. Miller's foundational beliefs is that education is a mandate, not a request. Thus, he has done extensive work in online higher education to develop systems of online instructional delivery, which embed accommodations and differentiation for at-risk and nontraditional learners without compromising the rigor of the course content. In particular, Dr. Miller has conducted research to inform educational institutions across the country of factors that lead to success of men of color in online educational programming. His research is currently being implemented in a major online university to rethink and revamp the academic, advising, and support services models in order to better facilitate success of men of color, and by default other at risk populations as well.

Dr. Miller's favorite saying is "Stay anxious to matter!"

CPSIA information can be obtained
at www.ICGtesting.com
Printed in the USA
LVHW030341151019
634227LV00002B/545/P